Educating Moral People

Educating Moral People

A CARING ALTERNATIVE TO CHARACTER EDUCATION

WITHDRAWN

Nel Noddings

TEACHERS
COLLEGE
PRESS

Teachers College, Columbia University
New York and London

Published by Teachers College Press, 1234 Amsterdam Avenue, New York, NY 10027

Chapter 2 reprinted by permission with minor changes from *Critical Conversations in Philosophy of Education*, edited by Wendy Kohli (New York: Routledge, 1995).

Chapter 3 reprinted by permission with minor changes from *Schools, Violence, and Society*, edited by Allan M. Hoffman (Westport, CT: Praeger, 1996).

Chapter 5 reprinted by permission with minor changes from a theme issue on "Rethinking the Social Studies," *Theory into Practice, 40* (1) (Winter 2001).

Chapter 6 reprinted by permission with minor changes from *The Construction of Children's Character*, edited by Alex Molnar (Chicago: National Society for the Study of Education, 1997).

Chapter 7 reprinted by permission with minor changes from *Elementary School Journal, 98* (May 1998). © 1998 by The University of Chicago. All rights reserved.

Chapter 8 reprinted by permission with minor changes from *Proceedings of the 1999 Annual Meeting of the Philosophy of Education Society*, edited by Randall Curren (Urbana, IL: Philosophy of Education Society, 2000).

Chapter 9 reprinted by permission with minor changes from the January 1995 issue of *Phi Delta Kappan*.

Chapter 10 reprinted by permission with minor changes from *Who Cares?* edited by Mary Brabeck (Westport, CT: Praeger, 1989).

Chapter 11 reprinted by permission with minor changes from *Journal of Moral Education, 23* (June 1994), published by Taylor & Francis Ltd., PO Box 25, Abingdon, Oxfordshire, OX14 3UE, England.

Chapter 12 reprinted by permission with minor changes from *Education, Information, and Transformation*, edited by Jeffrey Kane (Upper Saddle River, NJ: Merrill, 1999).

Library of Congress Cataloging-in-Publication Data

Noddings, Nel.
    Educating moral people : a caring alternative to character education / Nel Noddings.
      p. cm.
    Includes bibliographical references (p.) and index.
    ISBN 0-8077-4169-8 (cloth : alk. paper)—ISBN 0-8077-4168-X (pbk. : alk. paper)
    1. Moral education. 2. Caring. 3. Students—Conduct of life. I. Title.

LC268 N56 2002
370.11′4—dc21   2001053438

ISBN 0-8077-4168-X (paper)
ISBN 0-8077-4169-8 (cloth)

Printed on acid-free paper
Manufactured in the United States of America

09 08 07 06 05 04 03 02   8 7 6 5 4 3 2 1

To Steve Thornton and Lynda Stone—
wonderful students, cherished colleagues

Reason, being cool and disengaged, is no motive to action, and directs only the impulse received from appetite or inclination, by showing us the means of attaining happiness or avoiding misery: Taste, as it gives pleasure or pain, and thereby constitutes happiness or misery, becomes a motive to action, and is the first spring or impulse to desire and volition.

—David Hume

Contents

Acknowledgments   xi

Introduction   xiii

1   Care Ethics and Character Education   1

PART I: Moral Education from the Care Perspective

2   Care and Moral Education   13

3   Learning to Care and to Be Cared For   25

4   Care and Critical Thinking   39

5   The Care Tradition: Past, Present, Future   51

PART II: Philosophical and Historical Issues

6   Character Education and Community   61

7   Thoughts on Dewey's "Ethical Principles
     Underlying Education"   73

8   Two Concepts of Caring   85

PART III: Curriculum and Moral Education

9   A Morally Defensible Mission for Schools in the 21st Century   93

10   Educating Moral People   102

11   Conversation as Moral Education   118

12   Stories and Conversation in Schools   131

13   Looking Back, Looking Ahead   148

References   155
Index   165
About the Author   171

Acknowledgments

WONDERFUL CONVERSATIONS OVER MANY YEARS have contributed to the ideas in this book. I want to thank especially Larry Blum, Lisa Goldstein, Mike Greer, Marty Kirschen, Nona Lyons, Jim Paul, Rob Reich, Kathy Simon, Michael Slote, Hugh Sockett, Steve Thornton, Barbara Thayer-Bacon, Susan Verducci, and Marilyn Watson. Thanks also to many students at Stanford University and Teachers College for helpful comments and examples. My husband, Jim, has also contributed, as have my children and grandchildren, and students from my public school teaching days have left an indelible mark. As always, it has been a pleasure to work with the editors and staff of Teachers College Press.

Introduction

CHARACTER EDUCATION TODAY DOMINATES the field of practice in moral education. Disillusioned with Kohlberg's cognitive-developmentalism as a guide to practice and badly shaken by violence and disrespect in schools, teachers are urged to try character education. Teacher educators, too, are engaged in producing programs and curriculum guides designed to help teachers inculcate particular virtues. Even major professional organizations have launched programs of development on character education.

Character education has a long and checkered history as an approach to moral education. Its roots go back to Aristotle, and since that time, thinkers interested in moral education have argued over whether it is possible to teach virtues directly, as we do, for example, arithmetic. The question seemed to have been answered (in the negative) by the empirical studies of Hartshorne and May (1928–1930). Character education in American schools had virtually disappeared by the 1950s. Today, it has returned with great strength even though the questions raised earlier remain. However, it is not just the efficacy of character education that is questioned. It has been used for both noble and ignoble purposes. Fascist governments, for example, have used character education as a major means of socialization. Character education requires a strong community but not necessarily a good one.

In this book, I offer an alternative to character education. It is a sympathetic alternative in that the approach suggested (based on an ethic of care) has much in common with character education. Indeed, some writers classify care ethics as a form of virtue ethics, mainly because it rejects both Kantian principle-based ethics and utilitarian forms of consequentialism. However, the ethic of care (as I have developed it) is fundamentally relational; it is not individual-agent–based in the way of virtue ethics. The curricular and pedagogical recommendations that emerge from an ethic of care are more indirect and yet more pervasive than those usually associated with character education. Care ethicists depend more heavily on establishing the conditions and relations that support moral ways of life than on the inculcation of virtues in individuals.

The book consists of three parts. After an introductory chapter that outlines the similarities and differences between character education and care ethics, Part I discusses moral education from the care perspective. Part II explores some philosophical issues that arise in comparing an ethic of care to virtue ethics, utilitarianism, and Dewey's pragmatic consequentialism. In Part III, I turn to the practical implications of care theory for education and everyday life.

The focus in this volume is character education and care ethics. I have not attempted a survey of methods of moral education, but several works that provide an excellent introduction are available (Chazan, 1985; Heslep, 1995; Molnar, 1997; Nucci, 1989). Because the book is on moral *education*, not on moral *development*, I have not included anything like a comprehensive treatment of the developmentalists. Any educator who is serious about moral education owes a debt to developmentalists such as Kohlberg (1981), Perry (1970), and Piaget (1932/1965), and I apologize to contemporary developmentalists whose work is not cited in this volume. In studying the field of moral education, I have been struck by the vast range of thinkers who have addressed its big questions, and it would be impossible to include everyone who has made a contribution, without restricting attention to just one discipline. Such restriction would be a mistake for educators. Although we cannot study every discipline in depth, we need to be aware of major concepts and recommendations from education itself, philosophy, religion, psychology, literature, sociology, anthropology, and feminist studies. In this book, I have referred to work in all of these fields.

In the final chapter, I return to the issue of what to study and how deeply. I note that there are encouraging signs in a confluence of thought across several disciplines, but there are discouraging signs that we rarely talk to one another across disciplines. Thus ideas are developed in isolation. My final recommendation, then, is for greater cooperation across fields and more attention to the practical problems of everyday teaching. In reaching out to one another in generous conversation, we may also set the kind of example rightly expected of moral educators.

Educating Moral People

Care Ethics and Character Education

CARE THEORISTS AND CHARACTER EDUCATORS agree that the way to a better world is more likely to depend on better people than on better principles, but a question arises as to how we might produce better people. Care theorists rely more heavily on establishing conditions likely to encourage goodness than on the direct teaching of virtues. Neither group scorns fine principles, but history suggests that the prescriptive use of principles has not been effective. Moral people rarely consult abstract principles when they act morally. Both character educators and care theorists believe that moral motivation arises within the agent or within interactions. Our hope is that the behavior required by prescriptive principles will become descriptive of actual behavior. This is an important topic to which I will return in the last section of this chapter. Similarly, neither group rejects the use of reason or an education that helps people to use reason well, although care theorists may put greater emphasis on critical thinking (Thayer-Bacon, 2000). However, neither group believes that reason alone can motivate moral action. Highly educated people, well trained in the arts and skills of reasoning, have performed demonstrably immoral acts, and, in our own society today, many continue to do so. Thus character educators emphasize the inculcation of virtues in the belief that people of sound character will usually do the right thing without reasoning from a principle to a conclusion on how to act. Care theorists also have a healthy respect for virtues and their development. Indeed, we believe that children who are properly cared for by people who genuinely model social and ethical virtues are likely to develop those virtues themselves. This broad agreement generates the "sympathy" in the "sympathetic" alternative offered here.

Another area of agreement is found in the scope of moral life and, especially, of moral philosophy. The tendency since Kant has been to restrict the moral domain to consideration of our duties and obligations to others (MacIntyre, 1981). Like the ancient Greeks, character educators and care theorists are concerned with the broader question, How shall we live? The healthy development of oneself is thus included in a full discussion of moral life.

Character education has its theoretical roots in virtue ethics and recognizes Aristotle as its progenitor. Care theory, at least as I have developed it, is not a variety of virtue ethics, although it shares important characteristics with that tradition (Noddings, 2000; Slote, 2000). It is relation-centered rather than agent-centered, and it is more concerned with the caring relation than with caring as a virtue. Both uses of the word "caring" are acknowledged, and both are important in care theory, but the relational use is primary. In contrast to other forms of ethics, care theory credits the cared-for with a special contribution, one different from a reciprocal response as carer. Infants contribute significantly to the mother-child relation, students to the teacher-student relation, and patients to the physician-patient relation. This difference in emphasis—relation centered versus agent centered—produces concomitant differences in our views of moral education.

First, care theorists are wary of trying to inculcate virtues directly. As teachers, we are far more likely to concentrate on establishing conditions that will call forth the best in students, that will make being good both possible and desirable. This very important feature of moral education from the care perspective is discussed in some detail in Chapter 4, but readers will see its influence throughout the book. Second, care theorists are unlikely to identify seven or eight specific virtues to be inculcated absolutely or without regard to context. For us, virtues are defined situationally and relationally. The somewhat simplistic definition of virtues without consideration of context may be a defect not in virtue ethics itself but rather in the current popular interpretations we find in the character education literature. Third, care theorists may put far greater emphasis on the "social" virtues as described by David Hume (1751/1983). The reason for this emphasis is found in our relational underpinnings. How good I can be depends, in substantial part, on how you treat me. Therefore, virtues of congeniality, amiability, good humor, emotional sensitivity, good manners, and the like become centrally important.

Finally, in everyday classroom conduct, both groups make heavy use of stories. Character educators tend to favor heroes and inspirational accounts; care theorists lean toward stories that problematize ethical decisions and arouse sympathies. In this, we seem closer to Kohlbergian cognitive-developmentalists. However, we prefer powerful literature to philosophical fictions concocted as moral dilemmas. Here again, we exhibit a preference for broader, more diffuse conversation—discussion that will locate problems, not just attempt to resolve dilemmas. Moreover, the use of great literature supports our concern with social and intellectual virtues, and the stories thus chosen are valued for themselves, not simply as instruments for moral instruction.

CHARACTER EDUCATION

Contemporary character education programs, like their earlier counterparts (White, 1909), concentrate on the inculcation of virtues. Character is defined as the possession and active manifestation of those character traits called virtues. Thomas Lickona (1991) emphasizes respect and responsibility, but he also discusses honesty, compassion, fairness, courage, self-discipline, helpfulness, tolerance, cooperation, prudence, and democratic values. The program developed by the Heartwood Institute (n.d.) promotes seven virtues: respect, loyalty, honesty, love, justice, courage, and hope. William Bennett (1993) lists compassion, responsibility, honesty, friendship, work, courage, self-discipline, perseverance, loyalty, and faith. The Character Education Partnership (CEP) lists eleven principles, the first of which holds that "there are widely shared, pivotally important core ethical values—such as caring, honesty, fairness, responsibility, and respect for self and others—that form the basis of good character" (Lickona, Schaps, & Lewis, 1998, p. 1). The Giraffe Heroes Program (Graham, 1999) emphasizes compassion and generosity.

It is easy to be attracted to these programs, and, as I said at the outset, I have considerable sympathy for what they are trying to accomplish. But important questions arise, and character educators rarely consider them deeply. Perhaps the most troublesome question is one that has been with us for centuries: Can virtue be taught? (See Nash, 1997; Sichel, 1988.) In the Platonic dialogue *Meno* (see Cahn, 1997), Socrates raises this question and casts serious doubts on the possibility. But if virtue cannot be taught, how is it acquired? In a later dialogue, *Protagoras*, Socrates acknowledges that it must be learned and that teaching must be somehow relevant, but he is by no means sanguine about how this may be accomplished.

Critics attack character education on this issue more than on any other (Nash, 1997). The supposition that one can enumerate the virtues, teach them directly, and even assess the success of the process has drawn fire from several quarters. Hartshorne and May (1928–1930) studied the effects of character education in the schools and concluded that it just did not work; children subjected to such instruction behaved well while under the direct supervision of adults, but they did not otherwise display the virtues taught. More recently, Lawrence Kohlberg (1981) dismissed character education as the "bag of virtues" approach. His complaint, and that of many others, against character education was that it usually relies on indoctrination, and indoctrination is not an acceptable method of education (see Green, 1968). Thus the attack that begins with the Socratic question of whether virtue can be taught takes two forms: One challenges outright the contention that virtues can be taught directly, as we might teach arithmetic facts; the other objects that attempts to do so are forms of indoctrination, not education.

I agree that much of what goes on under the name "character education" is questionable on exactly these grounds, but the critiques also tend to be a bit simplistic. After all, as parents most of us do try to teach at least some virtues in a direct fashion. We say (and back up our comments), "You must not pick the kitty up by her tail; that hurts. Be kind." "You must not hit your little brother; be nice." "You cannot talk to Mother like that; be respectful," and a host of other comments that represent attempts at the direct inculcation of certain behaviors that are involved in, or may themselves be called, virtues. Are we miseducating when we behave this way?

Our judgment on the wisdom and efficacy of this approach depends on the age of the child and how we follow up on our initial commands. Even with very young children, most reasonable parents will add explanations to their commands: It hurts kitty when you do that. It isn't good to hit; that hurts. You make Mother feel bad when you talk that way. Of course, some of us make comments that may not be so helpful: How would you like it if I did that to you? Kitty will bite you, and it will serve you right. Nobody will like you. And so on, but the objection now has shifted to one against how we try to directly teach virtue, not simply against attempting it at all.

Parental lessons are usually delivered on the spot in response to a particular situation or occurrence. When teachers react in a similar manner, most of us do not object unless what they say or do is somehow harmful or unhelpful. Teachers, like parents, sometimes give explanations or make comments that run counter to their intentions to inculcate virtue. However, if the comments are congruent with acceptable moral intentions, we not only accept—we expect—that teachers will act in morally charged situations. But this on-the-spot correction is not typical of character education. Programs are planned in advance, and the virtues are taught out of context. It is this approach that can rightly be criticized as likely to be ineffective. That still leaves room for teachers, as educators of character, to correct bad behaviors and encourage those thought to be good. If critical work needs to be done here, it is almost certainly in how best to convey these messages so that children are neither shamed nor mired in guilt (J. Gilligan, 1992).

Direct instruction in the virtues may be thought of as a legacy from Aristotle (1985), whose virtue ethics is often taken as the prototype of character education. Aristotle defined virtue, first, in terms of behavior, second, in terms of feeling, and, third, in terms of reason. Children should learn to do what is considered good or virtuous, and when they are a bit older, they should perform such acts because the acts are good. When good character has been established, young people are ready to reason about virtue, to explore the reasons why certain acts or traits are good and others bad. Today most character educators would add reasoning, or thinking, to behavior right from the start (Lickona, 1991). The task for adults is to determine the sort of thinking appropriate at each age and how to encourage it.

There is another factor to consider when we think about using direct instruction on virtue. Not only must the situation be concrete and immediate and the explanatory comments helpful but also certain preconditions should be met. Children are much more likely to listen to adults with whom they have established a relation of care and trust. Character educators recognize this, but their attention to caring relations seems secondary; promotion of the virtues comes first. As we shall see, care theorists invert these priorities; caring relations come first, and it is thought that the virtues develop almost naturally out of these relations.

A second major feature of character education is its dependence on a strong community. The CEP principles, for example, instruct schools to state and describe their core values. To do this, a community must arrive at a consensus on what it values, and this is far easier for a well-established community—one with recognized traditions—than for a mere collection of people gathered together because their children attend the same school. Indeed, most people see this intuitively and worry about which subgroup will control the discussion. The question, Whose values? is almost always raised when a recommendation is made for character education in public schools. Obviously, this question rarely arises when the group in question is defined by, say, a particular religion or sect.

In Chapter 6, I look at the connection between community and character education closely. It may be enough here to point out that character education requires a strong community but not necessarily a good one. Fascist and other totalitarian states have been especially enthusiastic about character education, and schooling under such regimes tends to be highly moralistic, but not necessarily moral (Damon, 1988). It is a major problem for character educators (and for virtue ethicists) to show that their approach is not completely dictated by a particular tradition and that they can find a way to correct a tradition that has gone wrong.

A third large philosophical/social problem arises for character education and virtue ethics in the identification of virtues. Some contemporary virtue ethicists embrace a wide variety of virtues and even eschew a concentration on the so-called moral virtues. For example, Michael Slote (1992, 1998) prefers "admirable" to either "morally good" or "morally praiseworthy." One reason for this choice is to avoid the asymmetry of traditional ethics; that is, Slote wants to make vigorous and happy living for the moral agent as important as service and right action toward others. This choice brings virtue ethicists closer to care theorists; we, too, want to include intellectual and personality virtues in our catalog of virtues, and we mean to include them in our discussion of moral life.

However, at least among today's character educators, it is rare to find the inclusion of any but standard moral virtues. From the care perspective, the neglect of pleasing personality traits, admirable intellectual traits, and even attractive physical qualities (where these can be controlled by the agent) represents a shortcoming in character education as moral education. Because care theory is fundamentally relational, we recognize the contributions of the cared-for as well as those of carers in maintaining the relation. Admirable qualities of mind, body, and spirit all contribute to the health of relations and cannot be ignored in an adequate approach to moral education. It is much easier to behave morally toward agreeable, interesting people than toward nasty, dull people.

Two other problems arise in connection with the identification and description of virtues. For one, although we may all agree that "honesty" is a virtue, many (probably most) of us believe that there are times when honesty should be sacrificed in favor of compassion. Similarly, most virtues have to be assessed and ordered contextually. As children get older, they need to wrestle with the ambiguities inherent in the exercise of virtue (Damon, 1988). Character education programs tend to be better tailored for young children than for adolescents, and several later chapters will discuss this weakness.

The problem of virtues-in-context is exacerbated for many character educators because they fear and reject relativism. Without considering the high probability that they are themselves proponents of a particular moral ideology, they counsel against relativism (Lickona, 1991). But then, are we to assume that their recommendations are universally grounded? If so, we are left with the uneasy feeling that everyone else must be wrong. If morality is community dependent, must there be just one community after all?

In addition to the problem of helping children to activate a virtue that is appropriate for both context and community, character education faces a major problem in filling out a virtue—that is, in describing just what it involves. This "filling out" is often implicitly directed by the writer's or speaker's religion or philosophy. Lickona, for example, in discussing teacher responsibility, makes several explicit recommendations that from a different perspective might not be closely associated with either responsibility or respect: "high learning time; regular, monitored homework; frequent monitoring of students' progress in learning" (1991, p. 214). He also stresses a teacher's responsibility to keep students working up to the standards. Why should the assignment and correction of homework be listed as demands of teacher responsibility? Why should a teacher's insistence that all students meet a uniform standard be a sign of either respect or caring? In pressing such questions, we are trying to find out just how a given writer arrives at his or her interpretation of a particular virtue. This is another facet of the problem involving the denial of relativism.

A second, very tough problem arises within character education. Evangelical educators (Baer & Carper, 1998–1999) sometimes argue that moral virtues should not be taught in a secular framework. They insist that the goodness of such instruction is lost if God is not identified as the source of virtues. This is a position that makes it nearly impossible for public schools to do anything serious by way of moral education (Noddings, 2001), and it has led to the odd result that some parents actually object to the teaching (in public schools) of values that they themselves embrace (Bates, 1995).

Before turning to a discussion of care theory, we should say a bit more about the methods used by character educators. Some of those methods—banners proclaiming the value or virtue of the month, mottoes, competitions on virtues or good deeds—strike many of us as superficial and even counterproductive. Rewards for exemplary behavior have been challenged as likely to undermine the intrinsic motivation that should characterize virtuous behavior (Kohn, 1993). Acknowledging and complimenting generous or courageous acts may, however, be important. But notice, again, that the most effective compliments are likely to be sensitive and immediate: A caring adult notices and approves of what a child has done. It is quite another thing to set up a system in which rewards for appropriate behavior become an incentive for which children compete.

Programs such as the one suggested by Lickona (1991) emphasize the importance of schoolwide (even communitywide) agreement and consistency. I'm not sure that we can reasonably expect agreement on the definitions and descriptions of virtues, but it does seem important to convince teachers that the teacher is a moral educator (Jackson, Boostrom, & Hansen, 1993). This is not in itself an easy task, and many teachers insist that they "teach math, not morals." Then, too, consistency is not necessarily essential to moral behavior. From a care perspective, sensitivity to individual predicaments and encouragement are more important. Consistency on the part of teachers can, in fact, lead students to believe that they are "just numbers" and every day a predictable routine. This is not, of course, an argument for unfairness or capricious use of penalties. Because punishments and rewards are rarely used in the care approach, a lack of consistency is more likely to be seen as responsiveness and sensitivity than as unfairness. Urged on students as part of their moral education, consistency can encourage inflexibility and self-righteousness.

CARE ETHICS

Chapters 2 through 5 and most of the chapters in Part III will concentrate on moral education from the perspective of care ethics. Here, I just want to alert readers to the major features of care theory that make it an alternative to character education.

Earlier I mentioned the lack of faith both character educators and care theorists have in principles. It is not that we reject moral principles or find them less than admirable. It is simply that we do not believe they are adequate when it comes to motivation. On this, we tend to be Humeans: We believe that reason is (almost) slave to the passions. The educational task, then, is to educate the passions, especially the moral sentiments. Faced with evil, we must feel revulsion. Faced with another's pain, we must feel the desire to remove or alleviate it. Faced with our own inclinations to cause harm, we must be both shocked and willing to face the reality. Then we can invite reason to serve our corrected passions.

The Humean position is supported by some impressive empirical studies. For example, in their study of non-Jewish rescuers of Jews during the Holocaust, Oliner and Oliner (1988) found that most of the rescuers acted out of a group moral identity ("we are compassionate people, people who will help a sufferer") or direct care/compassion. Only about 10% said that they were moved by a principle.

I am arguing here about the power (or lack of it) of principles. Care theorists might accurately describe carers as operating so as to "establish, maintain, or enhance caring relations." But this does not mean that an individual in a caring encounter consults this principle before acting. Rather, he or she ideally acts in direct response to the needs of the cared-for. When this impulse toward natural caring fails, a carer draws on her own ideal of herself as carer. How would I act if I were at my caring best? This is just what many of the rescuers described by Oliner and Oliner did. They referred to a community of carers. I suggest that one can accomplish much the same result by calling on one's own ethical ideal as carer.

Another important point in care theory is that the emphasis on relation induces an accompanying emphasis on the conditions of moral life. One of the saddest comments I have ever read on school memories comes from George Orwell: "I was in a world where it was *not possible* for me to be good. . . . Life was more terrible, and I was more wicked, than I had imagined" (1946/1981, p. 5). Care theory does not attempt to develop a model of moral education that can produce people who will behave virtuously no matter how bad the world that surrounds them. We wish such a thing could be done. But it is part of a tragic sense of life to recognize that this is unrealistic, and insistence on trying to do it just adds to the misery of life. Instead, we concentrate on establishing the conditions most likely to support moral life. We want schools to be places where it is both possible and attractive to be good.

But don't we want the good habits and attitudes that develop in the supportive environment of fine schools to carry over into the far less perfect larger world? Of course. However, we recognize—and want students to recognize—that the potential for evil lies within each of us. If we are treated badly enough, we will betray our own ethical ideals, and even those we love. Orwell is helpful here, too. Remember what happened to Winston Smith in *1984* (Orwell, 1949). Threatened with the thing he most feared, he betrayed Julia, whom he loved. A thoroughly relational ethic emphasizes our ethical interdependence. We hope that children will overcome ordinary temptations, and now and then even extraordinary ones, but we accept the limits of ethical heroism. And so it becomes part of our everyday moral obligation to develop and maintain an environment in which moral life can flourish.

There are pitfalls here for the care theorist. We must not suppose that the conditions we establish can ever guarantee moral behavior. Character educators are right to emphasize the moral freedom that manifests itself in both heroism and villainy. Years ago, as a high school math teacher, I devised a system in which students could (within marking-period limits) take tests when they felt ready and repeat them as often as necessary. Math anxiety and test anxiety were both much relieved. Reasons for cheating were, I thought, eliminated. And still, two very good students cheated. I was dismayed to the point of tears, feeling both shaken and betrayed. But it was an important lesson. We are, I believe, at least in part responsible for the behavior of others whose lives we affect, but we can never be fully responsible. Each person bears responsibility for his or her own acts. In that, character educators are right. But care theorists are right, too, in working toward a world in which it is possible for the majority of people to be good.

Our use of stories builds on this basic understanding. Of course, stories may be inspirational, and they may portray heroes. But, more important, stories may help us to understand what happens—why people who are usually good sometimes give way to temptation or even evil, how whole tribes or nations can go wrong, how we are led to betray our friends out of fear, how we try to be good and become confused over what "good" means, how thoroughly dependent on one another we are for our moral goodness.

If there is a virtue that we hope to develop through stories, it is sympathy, intelligently guided by moral understanding (Thayer-Bacon, 2000). We put great emphasis on self-understanding and critical appreciation of the groups to which we belong.

Next, our emphasis is more on encounter and response than on community. We recognize the power and attractiveness of community, but we also observe the dark side of community (see Chapter 6). Community is by its very nature both inclusive ("us") and exclusive ("them"). In our emphasis on encounter, we agree with Emmanuel Levinas (1989) that caring arises (if we let it) out of the need of the other. The desire for some positive response presents itself on the face of the other. Caring is not confined to a group with identifiably common features. It recognizes the "community of those who have nothing in common" (Lingis, 1994). We should be able to respond to the pain of strangers as well as that of friends.

Finally, care theory has its practical roots in women's history and traditions. To say this is not to defend essentialism. I have no idea whether women are, by nature, more caring than men. I doubt it. But I do believe that much can be learned by studying the tradition of care that has been so much a part of women's history. Because it arose under conditions of subordination is not a reason to reject it but rather to assess it, cherish its best features, and encourage both girls and boys to enter its spirit and practice.

Moral Education from the Care Perspective

Care and Moral Education

INCREASED INTEREST IN MORAL EDUCATION in the past few years has led to vigorous debate among moral educators. In addition to the ongoing dialogue between cognitive developmentalism and character education (Nucci, 1989), the ethic of care has been introduced as a perspective on moral education (Noddings, 1984, 1989, 1992). Because the ethic of care has roots in both feminism and pragmatic naturalism, and because moral education is at its very heart, it holds interest for educators as well as philosophers.

AN ETHIC OF CARE AND ITS SOURCE

Like deontological ethics—ethics of duty and right—the ethic of care speaks of obligation. A sense that "I must" do something arises when others address us. This "I must" is induced in direct encounter, in preparation for response. Sometime we, as carers, attend and respond because we want to; we love the ones who address us or have sufficient positive regard for them, or the request is so consonant with ordinary life that no inner conflict occurs. In a similar fashion, the recipients of such care may respond in a way that shows us that our caring has been received. When this happens, we say that the relation, episode, or encounter is one of natural caring. The "I must" expresses a desire or inclination—not a recognition of duty.

At other times, the initial "I must" is met by internal resistance. Simultaneously, we recognize the other's need and we resist; for some reason— the other's unpleasantness, our own fatigue, the magnitude of the need— we do not want to respond as carers. In such instances, we have to draw on ethical caring; we have to ask ourselves how we would behave if this other were pleasanter or were someone we loved, if we were not tired, if the need were not so great. In doing this, we draw upon an ethical ideal— a set of memories of caring and being cared for that we regard as manifestations of our best selves and relations. We summon what we need to maintain the original "I must."

Now why should we do this? Why, that is, do we recognize an obligation to care? If we were Kantians, we would trace our obligation to reason, to a commitment that logic will not allow us to escape. But in the ethic of care we accept our obligation because we value the relatedness of natural caring. Ethical caring is always aimed at establishing, restoring, or enhancing the kind of relation in which we respond freely because we want to do so.

An ethic of care does not eschew logic and reasoning. When we care, we must employ reasoning to decide what to do and how best to do it. We strive for competence because we want to do our best for those we care for. But reason is not what motivates us. It is feeling with and for the other that motivates us in natural caring. In ethical caring, this feeling is subdued, and so it must be augmented by a feeling for our own ethical selves.

Kant subordinated feeling to reason. He insisted that only acts done out of duty to carefully reasoned principle are morally worthy. Love, feeling, and inclination are all supposed by Kant to be untrustworthy. An ethic of care inverts these priorities. The preferred state is natural caring; ethical caring is invoked to restore it. This inversion of priority is one great difference between Kantian ethics and the ethic of care.

Another difference is anchored in feminist perspectives. An ethic of care is thoroughly relational. It is the *relation* to which we point when we use the adjective "caring." A relation may fail to be one of caring because the carer fails to be attentive or, having attended, rejects the "I must" and refuses to respond. Or, it may fail because the cared-for is unable or unwilling to respond; he or she does not receive the efforts of the carer, and therefore caring is not completed. Or finally, both carer and cared-for may try to respond appropriately, but some condition prevents completion; perhaps there has been too little time for an adequate relation to develop. and the carer aims rather wildly at what he or she thinks the cared-for needs. A relational interpretation of caring pushes us to look not only at moral agents but also at the recipients of their acts and the conditions under which the parties interact.

Of course, we do often use the adjective "caring" to refer to people who habitually care. There are people who attend and respond to others regularly and who have such a well-developed capacity to care that they can establish caring relations in even the most difficult situations. But at bottom, the ethic of care should not be thought of as an ethic of virtue. Certainly, people who care in given situations exercise virtues, but if they begin to concentrate on their own character or virtue, the cared-for may feel put off. The cared-for is no longer the focus of attention. Rather, a virtue—being patient, or generous, or cheerful—has become the focus, and the relation of caring itself becomes at risk.

From this very brief exposition of an ethic of care, we can see that moral education is at its very heart. We learn first how to be cared for, how to respond to loving efforts at care in a way that supports those efforts. An infant learns to smile at its caregiver, and this response so delights the caregiver that he or she seeks greater competence in producing smiles. Caregiver and cared-for enter a mutually satisfying relation. Later, the child learns to care for others—to comfort a crying baby, pet a kitten, pat a sad or tired mother with a murmured, "Poor Mommy."

The source of our adult caring is thus twofold. Because we (lucky ones) have been immersed in relations of care since birth, we often naturally respond as carers to others. When we need to draw on ethical caring, we turn to an ethical ideal constituted from memories of caring and being cared for. Thus the ethic of care may be regarded as a form of pragmatic naturalism. It does not posit a source of moral life beyond actual human interaction. It does not depend on gods, or eternal verities, or an essential human nature, or postulated underlying structures of human consciousness. Even its relational ontology points to something observable in this world—the fact that "I" am defined in relation, that none of us could be an "individual," or a "person," or an entity recognizably human if we were not in relation.

It is obvious, then, that if we value relations of care, we must care for our children and teach them how to receive and give care. Further, our obligation does not end with the moral education of children. Contrary to Kant, who insisted that each person's moral perfection is his or her own project, we remain at least partly responsible for the moral development of each person we encounter. How I treat you may bring out the best or worst in you. How you behave may provide a model for me to grow and become better than I am. Whether I can become and remain a caring person—one who enters regularly into caring relations—depends in large part on how you respond to me. Further, ethical caring requires reflection and self-understanding. We need to understand our own capacities and how we are likely to react in various situations. We need to understand our own evil and selfish tendencies as well as our good and generous ones. Hence moral education is an essential part of an ethic of care, and much of moral education is devoted to the understanding of self and others.

THE COMPONENTS OF MORAL EDUCATION

Modeling, the first component of moral education in the care perspective, is important in almost every form of moral education. In the character education tradition, for example, it is central because exemplars constitute the very foundation of moral philosophy (Aristotle, 1985). In the care perspective, we have to show in our modeling what it means to care.

There is a danger in putting too much emphasis on the modeling component of caring. When we focus on ourselves as models, we are distracted from the cared-for; the same peculiar distraction occurs, as we have seen, when we concentrate on our own exercise of virtue. Usually, we present the best possible model when we care unselfconsciously, as a way of being in the world. When we do reflect, our attention should be on the relation between us and the cared-for: Is our response adequate? Could we put what we have said better? Has our act helped or hindered?

But sometimes we must focus on ourselves as models of caring. When we show a small girl how to handle a pet, for example, our attention may be only peripherally on the pet. Our focal attention is on the little girl and whether she is learning from our demonstration. Similarly, as teachers, we often properly divert our attention from a particular student to the whole class of watchers. What does our behavior with this particular student convey to the class about what it means to care? As I said earlier, the shift of focus has its dangers, and carried too far, it actually moves us away from caring.

In quiet moments, in the absence of those we must care for, reflection is essential. We should reflect not only on our competence as carers but also on our role as models. If I am, as a teacher, consistently very strict with my students "for their own good," what am I conveying? One teacher may emerge from such reflection satisfied that caring rightly forces cared-fors to do what is best for them. Another may emerge appalled that her efforts at care may suggest to students that caring is properly manifested in coercion. If the two get together to talk, both may be persuaded to modify their behavior, and this observation leads logically to the second component of moral education in this model.

Dialogue is the most fundamental component of the care model. True dialogue, as Paulo Freire (1970) wrote, is open-ended. The participants do not know at the outset what the conclusions will be. Both speak; both listen. Dialogue is not just conversation. There must be a topic, but the topic may shift, and either party in a dialogue may divert attention from the original topic to one more crucial, or less sensitive, or more fundamental.

The emphasis on dialogue points up the basic phenomenology of caring. A carer must attend to or be engrossed (at least momentarily) in the cared-for, and the cared-for must receive the carer's efforts at caring. This reception, too, is a form of attention. People in true dialogue within a caring relation do not turn their attention wholly to intellectual objects, although, of course, they may do so for brief intervals. Rather, they attend nonselectively to each other. Simone Weil described the connection this way:

> The love of our neighbor in all its fullness simply means being able to say to him: "What are you going through?" It is a recognition that the sufferer exists, not only as a unit in a collection, or a specimen from the social category labeled "unfortunate," but as a man, exactly like us. . . . This way of looking is first of all attentive. The soul empties itself of all its own contents in order to receive into itself the being it is looking at, just as he is, in all his truth.
>   Only he who is capable of attention can do this. ([reprint] 1977, p. 51)

The other in a dialogue need not be suffering, but carers are always aware of the possibility of suffering. If the topic at hand causes pain, a caring participant may change the subject. Dialogue is sprinkled with episodes of interpersonal reasoning as well as the logical reasoning characteristic of intellectual debate (Noddings, 1991). A participant may pause to remind the other of her strengths, to reminisce, to explore, to express concern, to have a good laugh, or otherwise to connect with the other as cared-for. Dialogue, thus, always involves attention to the other participant, not just to the topic under discussion.

Dialogue is central to moral education because it always implies the question, What are you going through? It permits disclosure in a safe setting, and thus makes it possible for a carer to respond appropriately. Dialogue provides information about the participants, supports the relationship, induces further thought and reflection, and contributes to the communicative competence of its participants. As modes of dialogue are internalized, moral agents learn to talk to themselves as they talk to others. Such dialogue is an invitation to ever-deepening self-understanding: What do I really want? What was I trying to do when I acted as I did? What good (or evil) am I capable of? Am I too hard on myself? Am I honest with myself? One important aim of dialogue with others or with self is understanding the "other" with whom one is in dialogue.

Dialogue as described here rejects the "war model" of dialogue. It is not debate, and its purpose is not to win an argument. It may, of course, include intervals of debate, and both participants may enjoy such intervals. But throughout a dialogue, participants are aware of each other; they take turns as carer and cared-for, and no matter how great their ideological differences may be, they reach across the ideological gap to connect with each other.

One organization that has put aside the war model of dialogue is a group of women on opposite sides of the abortion issue; they call themselves Common Ground. (Actually, several organizations using this name have sprung up around the country, but the one to which I refer here is in the San Francisco Bay area.) The purpose of Common Ground is not for each side to argue its own convictions and effect a glorious victory over ignorant or evil opponents. Rather, the explicit primary goal is to "reject the war model of the abortion argument and fully recognize that human beings, not cardboard cut-outs, make up the 'other side'" (Salton, 1992, p. A15). The women of Common Ground have described themselves as "frustrated and heartsick at what the abortion controversy has done to traditionally female values such as communication, compassion and empathy." But can an issue like abortion be resolved through communication, compassion and empathy? That question misses the whole point of the approach we are discussing here. The point of coming together in true dialogue is not always or only to persuade opponents that our own position is better justified logically and ethically than theirs. The issue may never be resolved. The point is to create or restore relations in which natural caring will guide future discussion and protect participants from inflicting and suffering pain. Many of the women of Common Ground continue their advocacy roles in antiabortion or pro-choice organizations because advocacy/adversary roles are the only ones widely accepted in American politics. But their advocacy is deepened and softened by the goal of Common Ground—to maintain caring relations across differences. Strategies that participants might once have considered against faceless adversaries are now firmly rejected.

Common Ground may well achieve desirable practical outcomes beyond a cessation of violence and name-calling. Already, women with opposing views on abortion have agreed on other goals: providing aid to existing children who are needy, helping poor mothers, defending women who are deserted or abused. Energies have been diverted from condemning and fighting to accomplishing positive, cooperative goals and, more important, to the establishment of relations that will allow ideological opponents to live constructively with their differences.

Talk, conversation, and debate are used in every form of moral education, but often the focus is on justifying moral decisions. Cognitive programs of moral education concentrate on helping students to develop moral reasoning. In sorting through dilemmas, students learn to justify the positions they take and to judge the strength of other people's arguments. It is certainly worthwhile to exercise and strengthen students' powers of reason, but advocates of the care perspective worry that students may forget the purpose of moral reasoning—to establish and maintain caring relations at both individual and societal levels. Of course, advocates of a cognitive approach to moral education may deny that caring relations are central to moral reasoning. They may argue, instead, that the purpose of moral reasoning is to figure out what is right. This involves an evaluation of principles and selection of the one that should guide moral action. If this were done regularly by everyone, they might argue, we would achieve a just society and reduce individual suffering considerably. But care advocates worry about principles chosen and decisions made in abstract isolation, and we worry, too, about the assumption that what is right can be determined in the abstract, logically, without hearing what others are actually going through.

The theoretical differences between care and justice perspectives are too many and too deep to explore here (see Katz, Noddings, & Strike, 1999). However, one point is especially relevant to the present discussion. There is some evidence that students exposed to cognitive approaches often come to believe that almost any decision can be justified, that the strength of their arguments is what really counts. Cognitivist educators are not happy with this result, but to change it, they have to lead students toward concepts that help to anchor their thinking. They usually depend on a procedural mechanism to determine right or wrong. Care theorists more often line up with consequentialists here. In trying to figure out what is right, we have to find out what is good for the people involved. But this does not make us utilitarians, either. We do not posit one stable, abstract, universal good and try to produce that for the greatest number. Rather, we must work to determine what is good for this person or these people in this situation and how our proposed action will affect all of those in the network of care. Dialogue is the means through which we learn what the other wants and needs, and it is also the means by which we monitor the effects of our acts. We ask, "What are you going through?" before we act, as we act, and after we act. It is our way of being in relation.

A third component of moral education in the care perspective is practice. One must work at developing the capacity for interpersonal attention. Simone Weil thought that this capacity could be developed through the "right use of school studies"—especially subjects like geometry. But all of us know people who are wonderfully attentive in an intellectual field and almost totally insensitive to people and their needs. To develop the capacity to care, one must engage in caregiving activities.

In almost all cultures, women seem to develop the capacity to care more often and more deeply than men. Most care theorists do not believe that this happens because of something innate or essential in women. We believe that it happens because girls are expected to care for people, and boys are too often relieved of this expectation. Whether or not the tendency to care is an essentially female characteristic is an open question, of course, but the hope of moral educators is that both sexes can learn to care. Indeed, most care theorists oppose any position that restricts caring to women because it would tend to encourage the exploitation of women and undermine our efforts at moral education. Caring is not just for women, nor is it a way of being reserved for private life.

What sort of practice should children have? It seems reasonable to suggest that just as we now want girls to have mathematical and scientific experience, we should want boys to have caregiving experience. Boys, like girls, should attend to the needs of guests, care for smaller children, perform housekeeping chores, and the like. The supposition, from a care perspective, is that the closer we are to the intimate physical needs of life, the more likely we are to understand its fragility and to feel the pangs of the inner "I must"—that stirring of the heart that moves us to respond to one another.

Similarly, in schools, students should be encouraged to work together, to help one another—not just to improve academic performance, but to gain competence in caring. Teachers have a special responsibility to convey the moral importance of cooperation to their students. Small-group methods that involve intergroup competition should be monitored closely. Competition can be fun, and insisting that it has no place whatever in cooperative arrangements leads us into unnecessary confrontation. But, if competition induces insensitive interactions, teachers should draw this to the attention of their students and suggest alternative strategies. Such discussions can lead to interesting and fruitful analyses of competition at other levels of society.

Many independent high schools and some public ones have begun to require community service as a means of giving their students practice in caring. But a community service requirement cannot guarantee that students will care, any more than the requirement to take algebra can ensure that students will *learn* algebra in any meaningful way. Community service must be taken seriously as an opportunity to practice caring. Students must be placed in sites congenial to their interests and capacities. The people from whom they are to learn must model caring effectively, and this means that they must be capable of shifting their attention gently and sensitively from those they are caring for to those they are teaching. Students should also participate in a regular seminar at which they can engage in dialogue about their practice.

The last component of moral education from the care perspective is confirmation. To confirm others is to bring out the best in them (Buber, 1958/1970). When someone commits an uncaring or unethical act (judged, of course, from our own perspective), we respond—if we are engaging in confirmation—by attributing the best possible motive consonant with reality. By starting this way, we draw the cared-for's attention to his or her better self. We confirm the other by showing that we believe the act in question is not a full reflection of the one who committed it.

In the ethic of care, confirmation is very different from the pattern we find in many forms of religious education: accusation, confession, forgiveness, and penance. Accusation tends to drive carer and cared-for apart; it may thereby weaken the relation. Confession and forgiveness suggest a relation of authority and subordinate and may prevent transgressors from taking full responsibility for their acts. Further, confession and forgiveness can be ritualized. When this happens, there is no genuine dialogue. What happens does not depend on the relation between carer and cared-for, and the interaction is not aimed at strengthening the relation. Hence it has little effect on the construction of an ethical ideal in either carer or cared-for, since such an ideal is composed reflectively from memories of caring and being cared for.

Confirmation is not a ritual act that can be performed for any person by any other person. It requires a relation. Carers have to understand their cared-fors well enough to know what it is they are trying to accomplish. Attributing the best possible motive consonant with reality requires knowledge of that reality. We cannot just pull a motive out of thin air. When we identify a motive and use it in confirmation, the cared-for should recognize it as his or her own: "That *is* what I was trying to do!" It is wonderfully reassuring to realize that another sees the better self that often struggles for recognition beneath our lesser acts and poorer selves.

PHILOSOPHICAL ISSUES

The model of moral education discussed here is based on an ethic of care. That ethic has an element of universality. It begins with the recognition that all people everywhere want to be cared for. Universality evaporates when we try to describe exactly what it means to care, for manifestations of caring relations differ across times, cultures, and even individuals. In roughly similar settings and situations, one person may recognize a cool form of respect as caring, whereas another may feel uncared for without a warm hug.

Because of its beginning in natural attributes and events, caring may properly be identified with pragmatic naturalism. John Dewey started his ethical thought with the observation that human beings are social animals and desire to communicate. The ethic of care begins with the universal desire to be cared for—to be in positive relation with at least some other beings. We note that human beings do in fact place a high value on such relations, and so our most fundamental "ought" arises as instrumental: If we value such relations, then we ought to act so as to create, maintain, and enhance them.

As Dewey filled out his moral theory, he moved rapidly to problem solving—surely one aim of communication. As we fill out an ethic of care, we concentrate on the needs and responses required to maintain caring relations. The difference need not be construed as a gender difference, but it may indeed be the case that the care orientation arises more naturally and fully from the kind of experience traditionally associated with women. Dewey himself once remarked that when women started to do philosophy, they would almost surely "do it differently." This observation in no way implies that a gender difference must forever divide philosophical thinking. Mutual influence and critical reciprocity may produce models that incorporate elements of both perspectives. However, it may be years before female philosophies are themselves fully developed. Will we finish up at the same place by a different route? Or will even the endpoint be different? These are intriguing questions for contemporary moral philosophy.

Although there is an element of universality in the ethic of care, we cannot claim universality for a specific model of moral education. Probably all moral educators incorporate modeling and practice in their educational programs, but many would reject confirmation, and some would reject the focus on dialogue, emphasizing instead commandment and obedience. Proponents of caring do not regard the lack of universality as a weakness. On the contrary, many of us feel that insistence on universal models is a form of cultural arrogance. Here we differ strongly with Kohlbergians on at least two matters: First, we see no reason to believe that people everywhere must reason or manifest their caring in identical ways; second, although we put great emphasis on intelligent action, we reject a narrow focus on reason itself. It is not just the level and power of reasoning that mark moral agents as well developed but the actual effects of their behavior on the relations of which they are part. Moreover, it is not so much the development of individual moral agents that interests us but the maintenance and growth of moral relations, and this is a very different focus (Belenky et al., 1986; Gilligan, 1982).

Care advocates differ also on certain aspects of character education. Although we share with Aristotelians and others who call themselves communitarians the conviction that modern moral philosophy has put far too much emphasis on individual moral agents wrestling in lonely isolation with logically decidable moral problems, we also fear the Aristotelian emphasis on social role or function. This emphasis can lead to hierarchies of virtue and demands for unwavering loyalty to church or state. Different virtues are expected of leaders and followers, men and women, bosses and workers. Further, educational models tend to suppose that communities can arrive at consensus on certain values and/or virtues, and this may not be possible for any except strong, traditional communities.

Early in this century, the Character Development League sought to inculcate in all students a long list of virtues including obedience, industry, purity, self-reliance, courage, justice, and patriotism (White, 1909). Probably both Kohlbergians and care advocates would agree that schoolchildren should have many opportunities to discuss such virtues and that they should read and hear inspiring stories illustrating the exercise of virtue. But to rely on community consensus is to lean on a wall made of flimsy material and colorful paint. If we all agree that honesty is somehow important, we probably disagree on exactly how it is manifested and how far it should be carried. Whereas Kant would have us never tell a lie and Charles Wesley spoke approvingly of the ancient father's statement, "I would not tell a wilful lie to save the souls of the whole world" (see Bok, 1979, p. 34), most of us would lie readily to save a life, a soul, or even the feelings of someone, if doing so would cause no further harm. Indeed, we might feel morally obligated to do so.

From a care perspective, we might begin with apparent consensus but with the frankly acknowledged purpose of uncovering and developing an appreciation for our legitimate differences. The need to do this—to respond to the universal desire for care (for respect, or love, or help, or understanding)—underscores the centrality of dialogue. We must talk to one another. Sometimes we are successful at persuading others, sometimes they persuade us, and sometimes we must simply agree to go on caring across great ideological differences. Unless we probe beneath the surface of apparent consensus, we risk silencing divergent and creative voices. We also risk allowing a core of powerful authorities to establish a fixed set of approved virtues and values.

A central question in the current debate over the introduction of values education is exactly the one alluded to above: Whose values? One side would press for its own; another would press for consensus. Care theorists would answer, Everyone's. But, like cognitivists, we would subject all values to careful, critical scrutiny, and, like character educators, we would insist that the effects of our choices on our communities and the effects of our communities on our choices be taken into account. We would insist that our community—nation, town, classroom, family—stands for something, and we would attempt to socialize our children to the stated standards. But we would do this with a respectful uncertainty, encouraging the question *Why?*, and recognizing our responsibility to present opposing alternatives as honestly as we can. Despite sometimes irresolvable differences, students should not forget the central aim of moral life—to encounter, attend, and respond to the need for care.

This reminder is addressed to moral educators as well. Although we differ on a host of issues in moral philosophy and psychology, as educators, we have a common aim—to contribute to the continuing moral education of both students and teachers. With that as our aim, we, too, should reject the war model and adopt a mode of constructive and genuine dialogue.

Learning to Care and to Be Cared For

LEARNING TO CARE and to be cared for is a major developmental task. There have always been people—some of them highly successful in other ways—who have never learned to care for human beings. For example, the great philosopher Ludwig Wittgenstein said of himself that he needed love but was unable to give it. However, he did care deeply about human suffering. Today many young people not only fail to develop the capacity to care, but also seem not to know what it means to be cared for. Some confuse coercion with care, some deceive themselves that they are cared for in highly exploitative situations, and some have simply given up hope that anyone will care. James Comer (1988) has described the feelings expressed by inner-city high school students toward their teachers: "They don't care."

It seems obvious that for most people being cared for themselves is a prerequisite to caring for others. There are exceptions—some neglected children draw on a heroic inner capacity for care that allows them to care for others despite their own deprivation. Other children who have been well cared for nevertheless fail to develop the ability to care. But it is clear that our society might greatly reduce the widespread violence and alienation so characteristic of life in the United States by caring more effectively for its children. This chapter explores ways in which schools should be involved in helping children learn how to care and be cared for.

A CLIMATE OF VIOLENCE

Many publications today present horrifying statistics on violence in the United States. A recent *Carnegie Quarterly* report states that "nearly one million adolescents between the ages of twelve and nineteen are victims of violent crimes each year" (Hechinger, 1994). An American child is killed every two hours by guns, and thirty more are injured each day. The figures vary somewhat from report to report, but they are never less than appalling.

Sociologists, educators, and others who study the phenomenon of violence blame it variously on poverty, doing poorly in school, lack of social skills, hopelessness with respect to getting a job, the influence of television and movies, and a general failure of morals in society at large. School programs aimed at reducing delinquency sometimes target one of these presumed causes—for example, doing poorly in school—and try to prevent violence by removing the cause. More often, schools provide protection by installing metal detectors, hiring guards, and locking doors and fences. It is estimated that the cost of such protection runs to $300,000 per year per school in New York City (Hechinger, 1994).

It is not at all clear that violence prevention programs are working. The Carnegie report suggests that some are (Hechinger, 1994), but a recent *Harvard Education Letter* article raises serious doubts about all such special programs (Posner, 1994). The best course of action seems to be to transform the whole school climate. In a caring climate, in a "full-service school," violence prevention programs may add the skills and knowledge needed to resist particular forms of violence. Basically, however, students must believe that the adults in their schools and communities care about them, that their well-being and growth matter. Kids seem able to survive material poverty, and many can ignore much of the violence in the media—or at least keep its effects to a minimum—if they have continuing relationships with adults who obviously care for them.

LEARNING TO BE CARED FOR

One of the essential elements in learning to be cared for is continuity. All children need the security of knowing that particular adults will be a positive presence in their lives over time. They need people who recognize their vulnerability, adults capable of what Sara Ruddick (1989) calls "holding": "To hold means to minimize risk and reconcile differences rather than to sharply accentuate them. Holding is a way of seeing with an eye toward maintaining the minimal harmony, material resources, and skills necessary for sustaining a child in safety" (pp. 78–79).

Today, when so many children lack continuity in their family lives and when conditions in the larger society exacerbate the need for continuity, schools must give greater attention to this requirement. Teachers, like good parents, must engage in holding. There is no good reason why teachers and students should not stay together (by mutual consent) for several years rather than for the one year typical of U.S. schools. Elementary schools in much of Europe have operated this way for years. The hard work of getting to know 25 or 30 children has little payoff in one short year, but over several years a relationship of trust can be established, and teachers can talk to students in ways that would seem intrusive in shorter periods of time.

Continuity is important not only in the elementary school grades but also at the middle and high school levels. Here students see their teachers only briefly, and teachers often deal with more than 150 students each day. If math teachers, English teachers, and other subject matter specialists could stay with the same groups of students throughout their high school years, caring relationships would have a chance to develop. Many of the teachers whose students report them as "not caring" really do care (in the virtue sense), but the structure of schooling makes it impossible for the caring to be completed.

If we think seriously about the need of children and youths for care and continuity, we will begin to assess all of our educational policies in its light. Should we bus students in order to achieve the laudable goal of racial integration? Perhaps not. If our efforts are likely to destroy the sense of community and make it virtually impossible for students and teachers to form relationships of care and trust, we must reject busing. However, there may be ways to constitute racially diverse groups that will, by general consent, remain together in a given building even though some of the students must be bused for years, and there may be ways of compensating students and parents who are willing to accept this hardship. The important point here is not the particular solution but the commitment to find methods that will not jeopardize the heart of the educational enterprise— the relationship between teachers and students.

Now, of course, a plan to keep teachers and students together for several years will not help those students who are constantly moved from place to place by their families or social agencies. But the need for continuity remains. Under such circumstances, the school has to intensify its efforts to care. It has to work with social agencies to care for the families, and it has to welcome impoverished and often lonely parents (usually mothers) into its community life (see Quint, 1994).

The discussion so far implies a point that is often implicitly (or even explicitly) rejected by many policymakers and educational theorists: Schools must be thought of and restructured as multipurpose institutions. They cannot exist merely to provide academic resources. Many policymakers blame the academic failure of today's schools on the fact that schools must "do everything" in this troubled society and therefore cannot perform the task for which they were constituted—namely, academic instruction. I think this assessment is dead wrong. Indeed, the evidence suggests that schools that accept full-service, family-like obligations also do better academically (Posner, 1994; Quint, 1994). If we want children to learn how to be cared for, so that eventually they will have the capacity to care for others, we must make it a primary goal of schools to care for them.

Continuity by itself cannot guarantee caring. By insisting that students and teachers stay together by mutual consent, we reduce the likelihood that continuity will be accompanied by cruelty or neglect. However, a school dedicated to caring for its children must encourage continual discussion of what it means to care. Teachers must have time to talk with one another about the problems they encounter, and students must learn how to detect and appreciate caring.

In a phenomenological analysis of caring, it becomes clear that the consciousness of "carers," in moments of care, is characterized by two features. First, there is a special form of attentiveness, which I have called *engrossment*; this form of attention is acutely receptive and is directed at the cared-for (Noddings, 1984). Second, there is a motivational shift; the motivational energy of the carer begins to flow toward the needs of the cared-for. Children who are genuinely cared for learn early to detect these signs in adults around them.

For a relationship—even a very brief encounter—to be caring, the caring must be received. The consciousness of being cared for shows up somehow in the recipient of care—in overt recognition, an attitude of response, increased activity in the direction of an endorsed project, or just a general glow of well-being. This response then becomes part of what the carer receives in new moments of attention.

If this analysis is correct, it is easy to understand why so many students complain that their teachers "don't care." The structure of schooling, especially at the secondary level, makes it impossible for teachers to give individual students the attention caring requires. Furthermore, in attempts to overcome their perceived academic failure, schools have become more and more coercive with respect to what is studied, and where and when it is studied. We have already discussed the need for continuity. Because continuity by itself is insufficient to guarantee caring, we must also consider how coercion affects attempts to care.

As teachers and students study the nature of caring and the variety of its manifestations, both may begin to question the degree of coercion in today's schools. Should all students be forced to take certain subjects? Can coercion be a sign of caring? Many teachers insist that the coercion they exercise in assigning and evaluating work is indeed a manifestation of caring. It is "for their own good." Correspondingly, many students assess teachers' caring in a similar way: teachers who care will insist that their students do the work. However, we must press the analysis further.

Alice Miller (1983) has written powerfully on the damage that can be done by what she calls "poisonous pedagogy." Such pedagogy is rigid and coercive; it seeks to substitute the will of the teacher for that of the student. Throughout the process of "educating," teachers guilty of poisonous pedagogy take a highly moralistic tone, insisting that what they are demanding is right and that coercion and cruelty, if they are used, are necessary "for the child's own good." Most of us have heard from some teacher or adult, "Some day you'll thank me for this." In all too many cases, we accept this pronouncement (or reject it) without analysis or criticism, and then, as adults, employ the same line of justification in our own relations with the young.

With careful analysis, we can sort out the worst forms of coercion from more innocent ones. Where a task is clearly connected to a purpose espoused by the student, coercion is usually unnecessary. For example, students who move from standard academic classrooms to vocational classes of their own choice often show an amazing increase in motivation. Their teachers do not have to coerce and threaten them. But sometimes, even in their chosen fields, students will resist certain tasks as too boring, tedious, difficult, or apparently peripheral. Then teachers may have to say, "Look, if you want to become a carpenter (mathematician, dental assistant, English major), you have to be able to do this." Many times, as a high school mathematics teacher, I had to say to otherwise energetic and highly motivated students, "I know this stuff is tedious, but learning it will make the next material exciting and much easier to tackle." In such situations, we apply a reasonable type of coercion. We say, "You have to *if* . . ." That "if" is all-important. It calls on students to recognize and reassess their own goals. It reminds them that they have come to us with purposes in mind and that they have entrusted us to help them fulfill those purposes.

Notice, again, how important care and trust are in the situations just described. Because we care, we detect the reluctance of our students to engage in the given activity; we allow them to express their reluctance. But we teachers know (or should know) that the prescribed task is really important to the goals sought, and so we insist on its completion. If students trust us, they will usually accept such coercion in good spirit.

Not all forms of coercion in school are so innocent. In the form just described, students are allowed to express their feelings, and teachers take those feelings into account as they offer justification for their coercion. Teachers attend to both students' feelings and their objective needs. Simone Weil ([reprint] 1977) said that the form of attention required by caring or love is very rare. I am not sure it is rare; it is common, for example, in parenting.

A question we must put to ourselves as educators is whether this form of attention must be so rare in teaching. Why do we so often fail to develop it and substitute instead an almost self-righteous belief in our own authority and the goodness of our coercive methods? Open discussion and analysis of caring might yield an answer to this question and lead to the abandonment of unhealthy forms of coercion.

What are these forms of coercion that I have labeled not so innocent? Anytime we force children to do something that is not connected to their own purposes, the coercion is at least questionable. Sometimes it is easy to connect our coercion to a child's best interest, despite his or her lack of purpose or understanding. We forcibly keep young children out of the street, for example, and we force them to undergo inoculations and trips to the dentist. Even in these obviously necessary instances, caring adults allow children to express their reluctance and pain, and we sympathize as we coerce. As we force children to go to school, the coercion becomes more questionable, and when we force adolescents to take particular subjects in school, the coercion should definitely be challenged.

Let us consider an example. Authorities in New York City schools recently decided that all students must take algebra and geometry. The New York schools are not alone in this decision; districts all over the country have made similar decisions. In the name of equality, in trying to care equally for all its children, a district decides that all students—regardless of interest, purpose, or capacity—will take the course of study intended originally for those planning to attend college. The decision is meant to be "for their own good," but it suggests strongly that their own interests, purposes, and talents are not highly valued—that to be valued themselves, children must conform to a particular model of success. This kind of coercion is at least questionable, and it is the sort that should be the focus of lively discussion among both teachers and students.

Clearly, I am not arguing against all forms of academic requirements. If students have made a well-informed choice to pursue a particular career or goal, it is reasonable to require that they meet the standards of their chosen enterprise. But a requirement that assumes a particular goal without the consent of students verges on "poisonous pedagogy." Without listening to what students are going through, what they really want to know, we treat them as units in a collection and force them into a mold they resist.

Many educators of good will argue that adolescents of high school age are too young to make decisions about their career paths. "Suppose they change their minds?" is the question repeatedly asked. The well-intentioned implication is that if a student prepares for a trade, he or she may some day regret that he or she did not prepare for college, and so, in just the way we yank a toddler off a busy street, we assign adolescents to algebra and geometry—for their own good. What we overlook in exercising this coercion is that students following their own purposes learn a good deal not only about the subject studied but also about learning itself, and they may also learn something about themselves as learners. If they change their minds (as many people do), they will know better how to pursue their new goals, and they may well have greater confidence in doing so as a result of prior experience. Students forced to take algebra and geometry may or may not "be prepared" for college study. Many will fail (the rate in New York City even before the universal requirement was about 50%), some will finish with a credential of sorts but little knowledge, and some will actually be inspired and adopt the goals suggested by their teachers. This last effect could probably be achieved, however, without coercion. In an atmosphere of care and trust, students likely to manifest special academic interests can be informed, enticed, and encouraged.

Care, I would argue, requires attention to individuals, and individuals have different needs and interests. John Dewey argued the case this way:

> The general aim translates into the aim of regard for individual differences among children. Nobody can take the principle of consideration of native powers into account without being struck by the fact that these powers differ in different individuals. The difference applies not merely to their intensity, but even more to their quality and arrangement. As Rousseau said, "Each individual is born with a *distinctive* temperament. . . . We indiscriminately employ children of different bents on the same exercises: their education destroys the special bent and leaves a dull uniformity. Therefore after we have wasted our efforts in stunting the true gifts of nature we see the short-lived and illusory brilliance we have substituted die away, while the natural abilities we have crushed do not revive." (1916, p. 116)

The result of academic coercion, even the best-intentioned coercion, is often frustration and a pervasive feeling of "being dumb." These feelings play a role in triggering violence. If a youth's own legitimate interests and talents are not admired and encouraged, he or she may never really learn what it means to be cared for. All care then seems to be contingent and associated with psychological or physical coercion. Young men try to coerce sex from young women by saying, "If you really cared about me . . ."; women remain in abusive situations because they feel it is their duty to care, or because they have no sense of what it means to care for themselves; evangelical advocates of religion try to force others to accept their beliefs in the name of caring for their souls. Readers can probably offer many more examples. Certainly, these aberrations of care are not entirely caused by the school's coercive curriculum, but that coercion plays a part in the misunderstandings that arise, and it leads also to a waste of real talent and energy.

Teachers and students must be given time to discuss these matters. Whether they agree with my analysis of care and coercion is not as important as their addressing the issues and reflecting on them. Indeed, from the perspective taken here, teachers and students who know what it means to be cared for will resist coercive instruction or care, but they may respond enthusiastically to an invitation to join in the discussion.

LEARNING TO CARE

When we look at the world as it is today, we might well wonder why learning to care is not at the heart of the school curriculum. Humankind has not yet learned how to avoid war, or even how to resist the most familiar forms of psychological manipulation that help make war possible. Perhaps worse, we have not learned to give and receive the joy and emotional support that should be part of family life. Of course, these forms of learning—all forms of learning to care—are difficult. May Sarton (1970) has the narrator of one of her novels say, "Family life! The United Nations is child's play compared to the tugs and splits and need to understand and forgive in any family. That's the truth, I am sure, but, like every hard truth, we all try to pretend it isn't true" (p. 49).

Perhaps in keeping with this need to pretend, despite the fact that so much of today's violence takes place in families, schools virtually ignore family life and learning to care for intimate others. When schools do offer courses on the subject, the courses are considered frills, nonacademic additions to the curriculum. Completing such courses counts nothing toward college entrance.

Learning to care is not a sequential process like, say, learning mathematics. (For that matter, although schools organize the mathematics curriculum sequentially, *learning* math may not be a sequential process either.) It is probably true that one must learn how to be cared for and to care for oneself before learning to care for others, but the process is not linear. As we begin to care for others, we learn more about what it means to be cared for. As we learn how to care for ourselves, we become more discerning in assessing the efforts of others to care. Sarton describes an elderly woman, Jane, who has learned in old age to accept care gracefully. Her narrator says:

> I have learned so much from Jane over the years, and the last thing is this seraphic way she has of accepting dependence—it can't have been easy for a woman of her spirit. How does she do it? She floats—why do I say that? I mean she lets herself be carried by Hannah, yet never becomes a baby, the baby Hannah wants her to be. It takes wisdom to be able to do that with grace. (1970, p. 50)

Children today need desperately to know how to care for themselves and for intimate others. I think it would be hard to exaggerate the mistakes schools are making in this domain. Instead of helping students to identify and develop their own talents, schools try, quixotically, to prepare everyone for college. Instead of tackling the subject of human life and love holistically, schools respond to various crises with drug education, sex education, and violence prevention courses. Religious and existential questions are rarely discussed, and English teachers debate whether literature should be taught for itself (complete with analysis), for its contribution to competence in reading and writing, or for its great existential messages. Some actively resist the last. Even philosophy teachers often insist that they do not intend to produce better people by teaching ethics. "I'm not a moral educator," says the philosopher. "I teach philosophy." But cannot one teach philosophy or literature with the clear understanding that one's aim is to help students search for wisdom and for better moral selves? And cannot this be done without imposing a particular view of morality on one's students (Wilshire, 1990)?

It is not reasonable to suppose that the school curriculum will be entirely reorganized around themes of care in the near future. But such themes can be introduced into traditional classes with salutary effects. The subject itself may become of interest to a greater number of students, connections can be made with other subjects, and students will feel encouraged to explore the eternal questions.

The question Who am I? must be encouraged, and as students explore their own interests and capacities, they should be advised and supported. It is not enough to take a few aptitude tests (which are then ignored by the school placement process), browse through computerized descriptions of occupations, and have an annual talk with a career counselor—although some unlucky students do not get even this much help (Kozol, 1991). Someone has to care about the individual kid who is asking the question; someone has to be proud of the answer that is emerging.

But, in addition to the personal connection, self-knowledge can be encouraged in academic classrooms. For example, religious and existential questions can be discussed in mathematics and science classes. Through biographical and historical accounts, students can learn how great mathematicians approached such questions. Mathematics students can be asked to analyze Descartes's proof of the existence of God. If the proof fails, does this mean that God does not exist? They should hear about Pascal's alternative approach, too. Pascal, one of the founders of probability and game theory, said that we should wager on God's existence: If we bet that God exists and live our lives accordingly, and God does exist, what do we stand to gain? If God does not exist, what have we lost? Stories of this kind can enrich ordinary math classes and help students feel less alone in their existential struggles (Noddings, 1992, 1993). The great mathematicians become more human as we hear them explore questions about God's existence, the problem of evil, the Bible's status as historical record, and the nature of the infinite.

Teachers at a given grade level can work together to plan units of study that are intellectually rich, interdisciplinary, and full of potential for personal meaning. For example, while a math teacher shares Leibniz's study of God and evil, an English teacher might read parts of the Book of Job with students. A social studies teacher might help students explore historical views of evil and how people in various times understood and tried to cope with it. A science teacher might discuss ways in which social Darwinism replaced earlier views of evil while retaining the basic idea that the poor somehow deserved their poverty. Together, the team of teachers might guide students through such works as Harold Kushner's *When Bad Things Happen to Good People* (1981) and Elie Wiesel's *Night* (1960).

For students immersed in a violent society, the search for meaning is especially important. Just to engage in such a search is a sign of caring for one's self. Teachers who are familiar with the music and films that young people patronize can relate that material to the academically acceptable topics I have suggested. At present, however, we do not use even the academic material that is available. How many students ever discuss existential questions in mathematics or science classes (Simon, 1997)?

In learning to care for oneself, self-image and self-esteem are, of course, important. Current educational emphasis on self-esteem has become the object of both caricature (in *Doonesbury*, for example) and serious criticism. Critics are right to question some of the strategies educators use to raise self-esteem, but they are wrong to ridicule its importance. Again, educators have too often gone at problems of self-esteem directly, much as they have approached problems of drugs, alcohol, sex, and violence. A wiser approach recognizes that a measure of self-knowledge is necessary for self-esteem and that there are features to deplore as well as to admire in most selves.

Adolescents need to understand how they seek self-esteem. Why do so many young men act tough? Why do so many young women permit themselves to be abused? Serious study of gender differences in self-image, and of how these differences are exaggerated and used by the media, should be part of the secondary curriculum. For example, students might profitably discuss the four basic rules of American manhood as described by Michael Kimmel (attributed by Kimmel to Robert Brannon):

(1) No Sissy Stuff: Men never do anything that even remotely suggests femininity. Manhood is a relentless repudiation and devaluation of the feminine.

(2) Be a Big Wheel: Manhood is measured by power, wealth, and success. Whoever has the most toys when he dies, wins. (3) Be a Sturdy Oak: Manhood depends on emotional reserve. Dependability in a crisis requires that men not reveal their feelings. (4) Give 'em Hell: Exude an aura of manly daring and aggression. Go for it. Take risks. (1993, p. 123)

A unit of study that begins with this paragraph might be followed by books, films, and personal accounts that describe very different pictures of manhood—some that illustrate the rules Kimmel criticizes and others that signify a modification of the rules.

Both girls and boys need to understand the social construction of femininity, too. Several of the female writers in the volume containing Kimmel's chapter emphasized the need for women to develop a vocabulary of resistance. Louise Erdrich puts the point this way:

To hold the *no* in my mouth like a gold coin, something valued, something possible. To teach the *no* to our own daughters. To value their *no* more than their compliant yes. To celebrate *no*. To hold the word *no* in your fist and refuse to give it up. To support the boy who says *no* to violence, the girl who will not be violated, the woman who says *no, no, no*. (1993, p. 338)

bell hooks (1993) and Ntozake Shange (1993) express the same point in ways particularly powerful for Black youth. hooks refers to "the dick thing"—the idea celebrated in parts of Black culture that to prove his manhood, a man has "to rape and assault black women and brag about it" (p. 153). She reminds Black women that they play a role in maintaining this attitude when they favor brothers who fit the image. Shange tells a wonderful story in which "mandy" teaches "ezra" a thing or two about resistance and the language of consent. Fighting ezra off both physically and verbally, resisting her own contradictory physical desire, mandy sets her house in order. At the end of the story, "there are no more assumptions in the house" (1993, p. 373).

The pursuit of self-knowledge—knowledge of the self as an individual, as a male or female, as a member of a race and community, as part of a particular age group—blends easily into a study of relations with others. Part of learning to care for one's self is a concomitant learning to care for others.

Schools can encourage this learning by providing a climate of care and trust as described earlier. Within that climate, teachers can use pedagogical strategies, such as cooperative learning, noncompetitive grading, and service learning. But, again, the strategies by themselves will not accomplish the learning we seek. The strategies have to be part of a dedicated drive to produce caring, competent, loving, and lovable people.

This dedicated drive should guide everything we do in schools. As we have seen, it should influence the structure of schooling by maintaining continuity of people and place; it should suggest an emphasis on teacher-student relationships; it should affect how parents and other community members are received in classrooms; and it should transform the curriculum.

How might the curriculum be transformed? We have already considered topics that might be introduced to aid students in their search for self-knowledge. As we assist them in learning to care for others, further topics may be studied. I will briefly consider three such topics here.

Consider love. Here is a topic that fascinates most teenagers, and teachers could construct wonderful interdisciplinary units on it. For those who worry about intellectual rigor, it may be important to include the poetry of the Brownings, *Romeo and Juliet*, *The Scarlet Letter*, *Wuthering Heights*, the biographies of John and Abigail Adams and Marie and Pierre Curie, and perhaps even *The Mill on the Floss*. I would not insist on any of these—especially not on *The Scarlet Letter* or *The Mill on the Floss*—if students show signs of hating to read as a result of their encounters with these books. Students could also see great films and listen to Berlioz's *Romeo and Juliet*, Wagner's *Tristan and Isolde*, Bernstein's *West Side Story*, and Gershwin's *Porgy and Bess*. Students could also study patterns of love and marriage in different times and places. The topic can be as intellectually rich as we care to make it, but the important point from the perspective of our dedicated purpose is that it is existentially rich. It connects to our lived experience and not just our conceptual experience.

A valuable exercise for teachers planning such a unit is to create a network of ideas and resources connecting the present topic, love, with another, say, violence, since that is our interest here. How are love and violence connected in *Romeo and Juliet*? Concepts that might emerge include hatred, feuds, honor, despair, suicide, and regret, and each of these concepts can be filled out with further reading and study. How are feuds and honor connected to violence?—if the school in which the teachers work has gangs, a new unit may emerge rapidly. Similarly, if there have been suicides or attempted suicides, planning may turn in that direction. *The Scarlet Letter* might suggest adultery, compassion (and lack of it), fidelity, and community prejudice. *Wuthering Heights* might suggest ambition, jealousy, passion, gratitude, loneliness, and mental health. As teachers discuss the possibilities, they may be amazed at what can be contributed by math and science teachers who are usually left out of such units.

Friendship is another topic that might be used to build an interdisciplinary unit. What does it mean to be a friend? How is friendship connected to violence? What do we owe our friends? This unit might begin with a newspaper article—one reporting how some act of violence was committed in the name of friendship, or how an act of violence was covered up to protect a friend. In addition to the moral dilemmas inherent in such stories, students might want to discuss friendships involving people of different races, ages, and sexes.

Again, the unit can be academically, as well as practically, rich. It can include a study of Aristotle's analysis of friendship. Especially important in that analysis would be Aristotle's claim that friends help one another to be better people. What might that mean for a boy who thinks he must cover up a friend's criminal activity? What might it mean for a girl who tolerates the abusive behavior of her boyfriend?

Literature can, once again, make a great contribution. Friends are usually drawn from a group of people like oneself, but occasionally incongruous friendships are formed. Consider Huckleberry Finn and the slave Jim; Miss Celie and Shug in Alice Walker's *The Color Purple*; Lenny and George in Steinbeck's *Of Mice and Men*; Jane and Maudie in Doris Lessing's *The Diaries of Jane Somers*. What characterizes each of these friendships? Can friendship be part of a personal quest for fulfillment? When might personal interest destroy a friendship?

A book like John Knowles's *A Separate Peace* can help students understand the forms of violence associated with friendship. Envy and misunderstanding lead the unhappy protagonist, Gene, to suppose that his friend, Finny, has the same competitive attitude that he has. In reality, Finny is innocent of such longings. What Gene learns from the tragic events that follow is that human misunderstanding contributes to violence at every level of human activity. Even war between nations can be traced to misunderstanding, to the narrow drawing of lines between people who perceive one another as reprehensibly different, to the mistaken notion that oneself and one's friends must be protected from these others. As an adult looking back on the events of his school years, Gene realizes that his schoolmates saw enemies and rivals everywhere:

> All of them, all except Phineas [Finny], constructed at infinite cost to themselves these Maginot Lines against this enemy they thought they saw across the frontier, this enemy who never attacked that way—if he ever attacked at all; if he was indeed the enemy. (Knowles, 1959, p. 196)

Finally, in transforming the curriculum toward one that will reduce violence and support a climate of trust and care, much more attention should be given to women's traditions. Teachers can draw effectively on women's traditions of care without claiming that women are inherently more caring than men or that all women are, by nature, inclined to care. Not all women have participated in the care tradition—any more than all men have participated in the military tradition. But there is such a tradition, and many beautiful examples can be drawn from it.

The tradition is illustrated in the character of Mrs. Shelby in Harriet Beecher Stowe's *Uncle Tom's Cabin*. Mrs. Shelby argues against her slaveholder husband that Uncle Tom and little Harry should not be sold. But she does not plead on the basis of an abstract argument in favor of abolition (which her husband is prepared to counter with a logical argument *against* abolition). Rather, she argues on the grounds of love and compassion. A tradition of care and compassion forbids an act that will separate mother and child, father and family. The tradition is illustrated not only in Stowe's characters, but also in her own life and in the work of her sister, Catherine Beecher.

The tradition we are talking about here has not been laid out comprehensively as an argument, and there is some question whether it should be. However, it is vividly revealed in the life of Jane Addams; in the novels of Virginia Woolf, Mary Gordon, Doris Lessing, Alice Walker, and Toni Morrison, among others; and in biographical accounts, such as Anne Morrow Lindbergh's *Gift from the Sea*. Pearl Buck's biography of her mother, *The Exile*, illustrates it again and again; we see an articulated Christian tradition and an unarticulated women's tradition, sometimes working together in charity, sometimes in great conflict where the first insists on adherence to rules of law and the second insists on responding more directly to human need. The women's tradition steadfastly opposes violence of all kinds, although its proponents occasionally fail—as all people do—to sustain their commitment. If we are serious in our own commitment to reduce violence and to help students learn how to care and be cared for, women's traditions of care must receive a prominent place in the school curriculum (Martin, 1992).

CONCLUSION

Violence has many roots, but it seems obvious that people who feel cared for and who have learned to care for others will be less likely to engage in violent acts. I have argued here that the first obligation of schools is to make care manifest in their structure, relationships, and curriculum. I have also argued that an emphasis on producing caring, competent, loving, and lovable people need not reduce the intellectual dimension of the curriculum. On the contrary, such emphasis should enrich the lives of both students and teachers intellectually, morally, and spiritually. As we begin the 21st century, we must make human relations the first priority of our intellectual and moral efforts. Schools can contribute by helping students learn how to care and be cared for.

Care and Critical Thinking

PHILOSOPHERS AND EDUCATORS have different interests in critical thinking. Philosophers are appropriately interested in how critical thinking differs from other closely related concepts (e.g., rationality), what it comprises (skills, attitudes, dispositions, and the like), whether its components are generalizable, and how its analysis fits with the traditional categories of philosophy, such as epistemology and logic (McPeck, 1981; Norris, 1992; Siegel, 1988). Educators, in contrast, are properly concerned with how their students use whatever critical thinking capacity they develop, with what it means for their lives. When the philosopher and educator exist in the same body, the educator—for moral reasons—should prevail. Thus I believe that we need to probe quite deeply into the connection between critical thinking and moral lives.

Before launching the main discussion, however, I want to mention a problem that faces us whenever we act as philosophical advocates for a concept that is intuitively "good." Jane Roland Martin (1992) pointed out this problem when she raised the question of whether critical thinking is always good or whether we might do better to recognize that it may be used, as Maxwell Smart (the comic secret agent in an old TV program) might have said, for either good or evil. Those of us working on the ethic of care face a similar problem. Should we define care so that it *has* to be good, or should we recognize and describe pathologies of care? If we choose the former, we find ourselves endlessly responding to counter-examples, constantly refining our definition and perhaps squeezing the life from our original concept. Still another example of the dilemma is seen in the currently popular idea of community. Many educators today see community as necessarily good. But we might do better to recognize the dark side of community and study it so that we can protect ourselves and our students from its worst manifestations. I think the better course of action on all of these dilemmas is to admit that there are problems and discuss them forthrightly. It is wiser, then, to admit that critical thinking does not in itself ensure either moral thinking or moral action. Our question then becomes, What can we do to encourage critical thinking that is morally directed?

VALUING A MORAL LIFE

Aristotle argued long ago that the only students who could profit from his teaching of moral reasoning and theory were those who already had sound characters and an appreciation for the moral life. For him, philosophical instruction required a starting point in a real-life appreciation that certain ways of behaving are virtuous and others are not. An understanding "that" certain ways are good must precede study of the "because," or why they are good (Burnyeat, 1980). How to establish this starting point for philosophical study was a matter of great importance among the Greeks. Aristotle, Plato, and Socrates seemed to agree that children need good models of moral behavior and that they should be instructed, if possible, to behave virtuously. Aristotle put greater emphasis on learning to be virtuous by behaving virtuously. Plato was so deeply concerned about providing good examples that he advised censorship of those poetical and dramatic works that might have an adverse effect on the young. Thus in classical Greek thought, we find two ideas that we will pursue further here: first, that effective philosophical study requires a starting point in real life and, second, that the arts can be a powerful influence on moral development. I want to take the same approach to critical thinking. Critical thinking, I will argue, requires a starting point in moral sensibility, and the arts can contribute significantly to the development of such sensibility.

Centuries after Aristotle, Simone Weil ([reprint] 1977) also sought a way of bringing students to a heightened moral sensibility. Her idea was that school studies should teach children how to attend. The capacity for attention thus developed could then be turned to God in prayer, and communion with God should produce moral concern for one's fellow human beings. Her reasoning is not confirmed by empirical evidence, and I think she was plainly wrong in making a fast connection between intellectual and moral attention. What seems clearly right, from the care perspective, is Weil's emphasis on attention and her identification of the question we met earlier, What are you going through? as a central question of moral life. Asking such a question fastens our attention on the living other—not on a set of principles or our own righteousness. However, the question still remains how to develop the capacity for such attention.

In our search for a starting point that will both enrich critical thinking and further develop moral behavior, we might agree that some consideration should be given to the development of virtues. I have recommended that adults should show children how to care, engage regularly in dialogue with them about care, and provide many opportunities for them to practice caring. In these recommendations, the care perspective resembles character education, but it differs significantly in its emphasis on the caring relation and its corresponding de-emphasis on care as a virtue securely attached to an individual. There are dangers as well as positive possibilities in character education. Forms of character education that put great emphasis on the norms of the community and/or personal virtue run the risk of producing people whose self-righteousness draws strong lines between themselves and "others" whose values and ways of life are judged inferior. Overly vigorous obedience to authority and hypocrisy may also result. Now, of course, I am not claiming that deplorable traits and behaviors are a necessary, or even frequent, result of character education. But it would be dangerous to suppose that instruction in the virtues would by itself provide a starting point for careful reasoning about moral matters.

To develop the form of attention described by Weil, we may have to cultivate the moral sentiments as David Hume (1751/1983) advised. We have to *feel* something that prompts us to ask, "What are you going through?" and we have to feel something again when we hear the answer, if we are to respond appropriately.

Hume suggested that stories and the arts help in cultivating the moral sentiments. They tend to humanize us and make us more agreeable. In his discussion, Hume draws on Shakespeare's *Julius Caesar*, quoting the bit where Caesar tells Antony his misgivings about Cassius:

> He loves no play,
> As thou do'st, Antony: He hears no music:
> Seldom he smiles; and smiles in such a sort,
> As if he mock'd himself, and scorn'd his spirit
> That could be mov'd to smile at anything.

"Such men are dangerous," says Caesar, and Hume comments:

> Also, having little enjoyment in themselves, they can never become agreeable to others, or contribute to social entertainment. In all polite nations and ages, a relish for pleasure, if accompanied with temperance and decency, is esteemed a considerable merit, even in the greatest men. (Hume, 1751/1983, p. 62)

But clearly there is no guarantee that love of the arts will produce morally sensitive people. People evil to the point of depravity have enjoyed Beethoven and Wagner. But Hume was careful to include virtues such as temperance and decency in his discussion. As we attempt to cultivate moral sensitivity through the arts, we have to acknowledge that other sentiments can also be aroused.

It is not surprising that educators have so often tried to avoid arousing emotions. Many have become afraid even to discuss values, and those who do engage in such discussion try hard to avoid indoctrination. There are good reasons why educators turned to the so-called cognitive approaches to moral education, and today there is increasing emphasis on critical thinking. But my claim here is that critical thinking needs a starting point in both character and feeling, and most episodes of critical thinking should be liberally sprinkled with turning points—points at which the thinker reaches toward the living other with feeling that responds to the other's condition.

Some years ago, in criticizing emotivism (a doctrine that describes moral judgment as strong emotional preference), C. S. Lewis made a similar point. Insisting that moral expressions are not simple statements of preference, Lewis recommended that students be helped to understand the significance of their moral traditions and that they be encouraged to feel something on hearing the stories that characterize these traditions. From his perspective, emotion is central to moral life, but moral life cannot be reduced to emotion; neither can it be reduced to rational thinking. He noted that educators at the time were trying to teach children to set aside their emotions and use critical thinking so that they would not be beguiled by advertising and propaganda. But, Lewis wrote:

> My own experience as a teacher tells an opposite tale. For every one pupil who needs to be guarded from a weak excess of sensibility there are three who need to be awakened from the slumber of cold vulgarity.

Further,

> by starving the sensibility of our pupils we only make them easier prey to the propagandist when he comes. For famished nature will be avenged and a hard heart is not infallible protection against a soft head. (1955, p. 24)

However, there are great risks when we attempt to satisfy "famished nature." The arts can draw forth both desirable and undesirable feelings, and we—the adults who are trying to draw feelings forth—may disagree vehemently about what is desirable or undesirable. For example, Lewis uses the story of the Roman father who taught his son that it is sweet and seemly to die for one's country as a powerful example that moral expression has substance—that it is designed to express and induce commitment, not merely to express a preference. Surely, Lewis is right that this particular story has had enormous impact on the practices of raising male children in the Western tradition. But is this the message we want to give? Is the substance—undeniably evocative—the substance we want to endorse?

Here I think we have an obligation as teachers to balance the account. I would certainly want students to hear the story and others in the same tradition—stories of great courage and loyalty, stories that induce pre-rational commitment. But I would want to alternate such stories with passionate accounts that take the opposite view. Much of the moving poetry of World War I challenges the Roman story directly.

Would I tell students that I endorse the latter view—that I agree with the view expressed in , say, Wilfred Owen's "Dulce et Decorum Est"? Well, I would not be like the teacher in *All Quiet on the Western Front* who exhorted his boys to join the army—who sent them out to kill and die and be maimed, "ardent for some desperate glory." But when reasonable people differ, when there is really an issue, I do believe that we have a pedagogical obligation to balance the accounts, even when we confess to espousing one side. Instead of shunning emotion, we have to tell stirring stories on both sides. This provides a situational starting point for critical thought.

I want to say more about starting points in just a bit, because I've used the expression in at least two ways. But, before doing that, I must address a worrisome problem. In suggesting that teachers have an obligation to present all sides speaking on an issue, am I suggesting that, for example, the Nazi side of the Holocaust be somehow represented in the history we teach our children? The idea is so appalling that, once again, we are tempted to flee from all emotion-laden discussion. But as the hairs on the back of our necks slowly settle, we should explore carefully what might be meant by including the Nazi side.

If by such a suggestion, we mean that perpetrators and opponents of the Holocaust should be treated as two groups of reasonable people with differing views, then I think the suggestion is truly appalling. But notice that it is moral sensibility that is aroused here and that makes the judgment directly. We do not want even to engage in debate with those who might try to justify monstrous cruelty and injustice. And we should not.

However, I believe there is a way in which the Nazi experience should be included in studies of the Holocaust. Students should be helped to understand how martial music, heroic stories of sacrifice for the state (or cause), fiery speeches, propaganda posters, and the like can be used to induce fierce commitment to causes that turn out to be evil. As a psychological study, that experience could play a vital role in promoting moral understanding and growth. To help young people understand how it happened that other young people, very like them, came to be dedicated Nazis is surely a significant task for teachers deeply concerned about democratic and moral education. I will return to this topic at the end of this chapter.

Let's turn back now to my use of "starting points." In one sense, I am using the expression in an Aristotelian way. With Aristotle, I believe that the rudiments of moral character provide a foundation for moral reasoning. But I would add to this a well-developed capacity for moral sensibility, the capacity for attention and fellow-feeling described by Weil and today's care theorists (Gilligan, 1982; Lyons, 1983; Noddings, 1984). Some, I realize, would include this capacity in character, but I think it goes beyond character into personality and is perhaps even better described, relationally, as a way of being in the world. Development of this idea would require that we turn from ethics of virtue to relational ethics— Martin Buber's (1949/1958, 1965, 1958/1970) ethic of response, the relational self and its place in ethics (Noddings, 2002), and perhaps elements of Emmanuel Levinas's (1989) face-to-face ethics.

The second way of using "starting points" is more immediate. I believe that if we are concerned with moral outcomes, most episodes of critical thinking must start with the arousal of feeling. We must care about the people, causes, and problems to whom and to which we will apply our thinking skills (Thayer-Bacon, 2000). Both senses suggest pedagogical tasks. We must ask how to establish the capacity referred to in the first sense, and we must press questions about the legitimate use of the arts in inducing the feelings that furnish starting points in the second sense.

THE POWER OF STORIES

Here I want to argue, first, for the use of stories in developing the capacity that might safely establish a starting point for critical thinking and the philosophical study of morality and ethics. Second, I will argue for their thematic use.

Several literature-based programs of moral education are now in use, and interest in them is growing. The basic idea is to choose literature of high quality that illustrates the virtues we want children to internalize. In the best of these programs, a teacher reads to children (or the children may participate in reading aloud), a virtue is identified, and open discussion follows. In one program, stories from all over the world are included, and children are asked to place colored pins representing particular virtues on a world map in the area described in the story. At the end of a year's reading, children should see the world covered in the core virtues.

At this stage—elementary school—educators wisely leave aside the fact that the world is also covered in evil (although that point comes through to some degree), that the virtues are manifested in different ways, that not every possible virtue is discussed, and that some virtues may be emphasized more than others. The idea is not to argue, refine, or justify, but to give children the thought/feeling that there is good in people everywhere and that people in every walk of life can exercise that goodness.

This approach to moral education, the use of stories, has a long and mixed history. Almost every form of religious education uses it, and parents choose it almost instinctively. The history is "mixed" because many advocates do not emphasize goodness everywhere but instead concentrate on the superiority of their own group and its values. It is also mixed because early exposure to stories of great emotional power has not often been followed up either by stories from the other side of an issue or by critical discussion. Indoctrination has been routine.

Even today, thoughtful developers of curriculum are under pressure to anchor their teaching in authority—the word of God, or the American way—and opposition to the "rudderless" way of teaching virtues is growing (Bates, 1995; Baer & Carper, 1998–1999). These opponents do not want their children to exercise moral imagination; they want moral conformity and obedience. What we see here—in both advocates of nondoctrinaire literature-based programs and their opponents—is general recognition that stories have enormous power.

Both sides also want to accomplish something beyond the starting point I have so far emphasized. The developers of Heartwood, for example, really do want children to appreciate and exercise the virtues exemplified in their literature. Critics on the Christian right also want this, but they want something more—they want their children to believe that the virtues can be genuinely understood and exercised only in a framework of Christian belief. Their message, quite literally, is, Teach it our way or don't teach it at all. This attack will have to be courageously resisted, and it will not do to give up the story phase and try to maintain the critical thinking phase, because the latter is empty without the former.

Consider, for example, the power of *Uncle Tom's Cabin*. At the time Stowe wrote her novel, debate (reasoned dialogue?) raged over the rightness or wrongness of slavery. Recall the discussion in Chapter 3 of the scene in the novel that illustrates the difference between a rational-feeling approach and a rational approach that has escaped the domain of feeling entirely. Mrs. Shelby reacts with horror to her husband's decision to sell Uncle Tom and little Harry. Her husband argues financial necessity. When that is brushed aside, he accuses his wife of talking like an abolitionist and reminds her that "pious men" have argued for the justice of slavery. Mrs. Shelby refuses the invitation to argue abstractly. There are loving families involved here—human beings she herself has come to love—who care deeply for one another. Isn't this enough to forbid selling them? Doesn't moral sensibility give the answer directly?

The novel is its own best argument. Stowe actually presented a brief formal argument against slavery as an addendum, a last chapter, to the novel. But scarcely anyone remembers the argument. What moved a nation was the story. Other examples abound; think, for instance, of the political storm set loose by the novels of Charles Dickens.

With such powerful tools at hand, we educators have to ask what we are trying to accomplish and how far we can go. I know that I, for one, want to do more than simply set the stage for critical thinking. Ideally, I would like students to emerge with a sensibility of care so heightened that to do deliberate harm to another human being would be very nearly unthinkable. Would we dare to work actively toward such a goal? Even if we promise to present the other side in all its eloquence (as I have promised), even if the case is ultimately presented in the court of reason, would we be allowed to work openly toward such a goal?

In a newsmagazine interview more than a decade ago, Elie Wiesel raised the question of whether we are afraid of peace. He pointed out that simulations and role playing (acting-out stories) are so powerful in promoting the moral sentiments that leaders of armed forces fear that such exercises might lead to a refusal to fight. In the interview, Wiesel said:

> If the soldier were to imagine the suffering he is ready to bring about, he would be less eager to wage war. If he were to consider the enemy a potential victim—and therefore capable of weeping, of despairing, of dying—the relationship between them would be changed. Every effort is made, therefore, to limit, even stifle, his humane impulses, his imagination and his capacity to experience a feeling of brotherhood toward his fellow man. (1989, p. 8)

When we advocate enhancing this imagination, we can expect to encounter resistance. Further, we have to acknowledge that we could be wrong. In any given case, we might be on the side that will ultimately be judged wrong. However, we have to embrace a way of being in the world that we will stand for devotedly even though we may make mistakes. I may, for example, in caring deeply, advocate nonviolence when a fight would better preserve those for whom I care; I might advocate action prematurely; or in reaching out to care for someone, I might inadvertently hurt several others. Because I could be wrong in a given case, I must, without ceasing to care, listen to others and exercise the best of critical thinking. It is in this area that I think Richard Paul's (1990) "strong sense" of critical thinking and Harvey Siegel's (1988) "critical spirit" have great power. But, at bottom, I cannot be wrong in choosing a way of life characterized by care, and it is that sensibility that we must be courageous enough to develop in the young.

AN EXTENDED EXAMPLE

So far I have argued that moral development depends as much on moral sensibility as on reasoning, and that the former together with the rudiments of moral character provide a starting point for critical thinking and the philosophical study of morality. I have argued also that the arts, especially literature, can be used to encourage moral sensibility. Now I want to offer an example of the kind of story and discussion I have in mind.

The following story is told by Simon Wiesenthal. We may assume from what follows the story that the young Jew in the story is Wiesenthal himself:

> A young Jew is taken from a death camp to a makeshift army hospital. He is led to the bedside of a Nazi soldier whose head is completely swathed in bandages. The dying Nazi blindly extends his hand to the Jew, and in a cracked whisper begins to speak. The Jew listens silently while the Nazi confesses to having participated in the burning alive of an entire village of Jews. The soldier, terrified of dying with this burden of guilt, begs absolution from the Jew. Having listened to the Nazi's story for several hours—torn between horror and compassion for the dying man—the Jew finally walks out of the room without speaking. (1976)

After the war, Wiesenthal, who had not expected to survive, goes to visit the dead soldier's mother and, without telling her of his encounter with her son or the confession he had heard, listens as the mother talks about Karl, "a dear good boy." She describes Karl's religious upbringing and how she and her husband lost him to the Hitler Youth. Out of compassion, Wiesenthal remains silent about Karl's confession.

Years later, Wiesenthal—still agonizing over whether he did right or wrong in leaving the bedside without speaking—gathers together a symposium of distinguished thinkers and asks them, Did I do right or wrong?

The question itself is typical of the traditional approach to ethics. Either answer, "right" or "wrong," demands justification, and although it is useful to engage in debate as part of moral education, such debate by itself fails to get at the deepest existential questions: Why do we harm others? Why do we fail to meet the living other with Weil's deeply moral question? Can we imagine ourselves as Wiesenthal? As Karl?

Most of the respondents were able to identify sufficiently with Wiesenthal to express sympathy and understanding for his predicament. Recognizing the extremity of Wiesenthal's condition and the horrors he experienced, no one on the panel was willing to judge him. Thus there was, at least initially, evidence that the panelists were sensitive to what the young Jew had gone through. But this approach was quickly put aside by most of the respondents as they turned to their own traditions, symbols, and moral codes to answer the question, right or wrong?

One set of responses focused on the religious requirement to forgive the truly penitent. Most respondents believed that Karl, dying in physical and psychic agony, was genuinely penitent; his remorse was not questioned. Therefore, although these speakers could understand why Wiesenthal was unable to do so, their considered judgment was that, if he had not been in such peril and misery himself, he would have and should have granted forgiveness.

Another approach centered on symbols. The two actual men meeting in a face-to-face encounter were forgotten. Wiesenthal became a symbol of all Jewry and Karl a symbol of Nazism. On this level, forgiveness was seen as impossible and even immoral. The last respondent, Friedrich Torberg, assured Wiesenthal that his failure to forgive was not a sign of moral failure:

> If today, after all your experiences you are still worried by the question whether you should have forgiven a Nazi murderer, that very fact is far more valid evidence of an intact morality than if you had actually forgiven him. It is in this intact morality . . . that we are superior to the others, to the murderers and to those who held their peace about the murders when they were committed and are still holding their peace today. (in Wiesenthal, 1976, p. 208)

Here we can begin to encourage the exercise of care and ethical imagination. What is this "intact morality" of which Torberg speaks and how do we maintain it? Surely, people like Wiesenthal, Elie Wiesel, and many others who survived the horrors of the death camps are to be credited with moral heroism when they emerge still able to care deeply for others. From the care perspective, Wiesenthal demonstrated his intact morality more convincingly in his compassionate treatment of Karl's mother than in his persistent concern to answer the question of whether he was right or wrong.

Can we imagine ourselves without an intact morality? On the other hand, is anyone really in possession of such a thing? We can readily acknowledge that we all make moral mistakes. In the language of religion, we commit sins. We do not really possess an intact morality if we look at our lives in a case-by-case examination. However, if we retain a way of being in the world that allows us to respond to the other, to ask, What are you going through? and to act compassionately on what we hear, perhaps we have come close.

Thus our imaginations are challenged with a series of questions. How can we maintain a moral way of being in the world? How do we live it? As we go beyond the debate on justification, what can we learn from Wiesenthal's story?

Probably most students, like the symposium participants, could imagine themselves in Wiesenthal's position. We can usually see ourselves as victims, especially if the victims are recognized as good and innocent. Wiesel's challenge is harder—to imagine the suffering one is about to inflict. It may have been because he knew that he had added to Karl's suffering by his silence that Wiesenthal agonized all those years. But Karl was not an innocent sufferer. Was his suffering deserved? (For an analysis of just deserts, see Noddings, 2002.) Should we cut the chain of suffering, deserved or undeserved, when we can? Some of Wiesenthal's respondents feared that forgiveness would somehow have excused the whole Nazi regime, that it would have betrayed dead Jews and those still suffering. But that fear takes imagination too far and in the wrong direction. Wiesenthal and Karl were alone. It was an encounter between two suffering young men barely out of boyhood. We need to think on this, to exercise our imagination on the possibilities. Can we live so that we help to cut the chains of suffering, enmity, and violence?

Now for the hardest challenge to imagination. Can we see ourselves as Karl? Most listeners and readers find this very difficult. Indeed, when I pose this question to live audiences, many suppose that I am pleading for an understanding of Karl that will arouse our sympathy and perhaps excuse his monstrous acts. But, although a form of sympathy may indeed be aroused, that is not the point. The point is to explore how a "good boy" became a Nazi. The point is to understand ourselves better, and through that understanding to provide a moral climate in which our children are unlikely to perform violent and vicious acts.

Could I have been like Karl? Most of us deny the possibility. But, for myself, I am not so sure. Having been a child myself in that era, I can imagine being dazzled by the snappy uniforms, colorful flags, martial music, precision marching, fiery speeches, and call to honorable comradeship. I—a child who adored her teachers—would have been especially vulnerable. If they had said, "This is right," or even failed to say, "This is wrong" . . . If I had been a boy . . .

What we see when we exercise the moral imagination is that a form of moral luck plays a part in what Torberg called an intact morality. I was not put to the test as Karl was. But beyond luck, there is responsibility, and the responsibility of parents and teachers is to provide the healthiest possible moral climate for the young. No child should be put to the test as Karl and his companions were.

We have now come back to our starting point. It is useful and interesting to study the Wiesenthal story critically—to argue the merits of forgiving or not forgiving, to endorse or reject the level of abstraction that turned Karl and Wiesenthal into "specimens from the collection" of Nazis and Jews, to argue for or against meeting Karl as a sufferer rather than a criminal enemy. All of this is instructive. But, at bottom, the story calls for an exercise of ethical imagination that forces us to consider the conditions under which we might lose our very way of being in the world. To respond to Karl's suffering is not to betray the innocent dead, nor is it to usurp the right of all Jewry to forgive or not to forgive, nor is it the formal application of forgiveness required by both Judaic and Christian law. Rather, it is to respond to this particular sufferer and, beyond that, to the suffering that accompanies recognition that our own souls (ways of being) might be lost.

When we imagine ourselves as victims, emotion is aroused, and that emotion may increase our compassion for other victims, or it may create hatred for oppressors, or both. Sometimes, in our horror of victimhood, we are comforted by the fact that we are not the actual victims; the actual victims are not as smart, not as innocent, not as blessed as we are. And when we look at the perpetrator, we are again comforted because we are not, could not be, that monster. But when we look at the scene of suffering and see *both* possibilities for ourselves, then a new horror is aroused, and that horror provides a starting point for morally directed critical thinking.

The Care Tradition: Past, Present, Future

THROUGHOUT HISTORY women have been charged with caregiving—with caring not only for their own families but also for the ill, elderly, and needy in their immediate communities. Such caregiving was universally expected of women, and those few who refused to meet that expectation were regarded as unnatural women. Today, when women in most Western nations have options outside the home and are no longer occupationally limited to the caregiving professions, educators face something of a dilemma. We want to educate girls for the wider opportunities now available to them, and we do not want to glorify a tradition that coerced and exploited women. But people still need care, and the care tradition is one that should not be entirely lost. Now both girls and boys should be educated for caregiving as well as breadwinning. This form of education should be an essential part of moral education.

For the past few decades, educators have been concerned with inclusion in a variety of forms. Here I will concentrate on problems of curricular inclusion, and in particular on ways of including the interests and contributions of women in the social studies curriculum. First, I will say a bit about the "add women and stir" approach that most of us now reject as inadequate. Then I will discuss the tradition of care that has long been identified with female life, and finally I will explore ways in which this tradition may be preserved and extended through a universal caregiver model.

ADD WOMEN AND STIR

When women and minorities started to object strongly to their exclusion from the social studies curriculum, the initial response was (perhaps quite naturally) to search historical accounts for the presence of women and minorities whose participation had somehow been overlooked. The results were in part positive, in part ludicrous. At least, women were now present, but it often required a stretch of the imagination to see *why* they were there.

In many situations where women now appeared, it was obvious that no white man who had participated so peripherally would have been represented in the text. Further, women often now appeared in illustrations but were still missing from the verbal text. We could count the number of female characters in a text's pictures, but we might fail to be impressed by any real female contribution.

The "add women and stir" approach was inadequate, but it was not all bad. At least it served to remind text writers and curriculum planners that women should somehow be included. It also contributed to a movement to provide opportunities for women. For example, if pictures of women engineers and physicians were included in text illustrations, both educators and students might well become more concerned with making these pictures real. Women would be encouraged to participate in professional and political life. It was one way, if somewhat strained, to break thinkers away from the "cult of true womanhood" and the notion that women belong in the home—their "proper sphere" (Kerber, 1997; Welter, 1966).

Another positive result of the search for women's participation in a man's world is still emerging. As the search has deepened and women's scholarship has become more widely accepted, we are learning more about women who exercised real power in the worlds of education, nursing, religion, mental health, and social policy (Becher, 1990; Blount, 1998; Crocco & Davis, 1999; Eisler, 1987; Reverby, 1987; Weiler, 1998). Women made significant contributions not only in these fields but also in science and mathematics (Rossiter, 1982). However, in all fields, but especially in the last two, their contributions were minimized and often forgotten in mainstream historical accounts (Noble, 1992; Rossiter, 1982). Clearly, it is important to search out and include the important contributions women have made in all fields, and these stories should be part of the social studies curriculum. The serious study of both significant female contributions and the almost insurmountable odds against which many women struggled is a far cry from the superficial "add and stir" approach, but it may have been given greater impetus by that otherwise faulty beginning.

We may raise another objection to the "add and stir" approach. It tends to reduce women to a male model and to obscure the contributions made by women who were restricted to the separate sphere of homemaking and private caregiving. Generous men from Plato on have made the mistake of supposing that equality for women must be measured by the male standard (Martin, 1985). How could one argue in the name of equality that males should be given opportunities to be more like females? It would be rather like arguing that we should achieve economic equality by making everyone poor! Students should be encouraged to think deeply about this. In what ways does the analogy hold? In what ways does it fail, perhaps tragically? Has women's tradition (if there is one) no special value?

A TRADITION OF CARE

It is undeniable that women have borne the larger burden of caregiving throughout history (Sommers & Shields, 1987). Even when individual women escaped the role of caregiver, they could not escape the expectation that they should provide direct care when the need arose (Reverby, 1987). Until the last few decades, women who rejected this role to pursue professional life were considered "unnatural" women, and it was rare for a woman to have both a successful public career and a (traditionally) happy home life. Students might be invited to see how many of the women identified as having made contributions to male-identified fields achieved this dual success. Sympathizing with, as well as admiring, those who have given so much of their own lives to care for others is a step in learning to care. It is possible, of course, that the effect of studying such lives carefully might be first sympathy, and then a vow to avoid the care tradition entirely. A mother I met recently was dismayed that her bright teenage daughter would not even consider teaching as a career. "I'm not going to spend my life helping other people to succeed," she said. When I discuss the future of care, I will return to this important concern.

Social studies teachers are often overwhelmed with the volume of material they have to teach, and what they actually teach hardly scratches the surface of what they might teach. When we think of women's stories, running parallel to men's and largely ignored in traditional curricula, we wonder how time can ever be found to treat them adequately. The admirable intention to include alternative histories often betrays itself in a dull hodgepodge of unrelated bits that satisfies no one.

Obviously, I cannot suggest a solution to the problem of curriculum balance and integration in this short chapter. But a reasonable start would be to launch and maintain a deep discussion of the aims of education. Why do we teach social studies? What do we hope our students will learn? What changes in attitudes, values, and cast of mind do we hope to encourage? Which topics, from the host available, are rich enough to contribute to the aims we seek? Social studies teachers, like math and science teachers, might do better to teach (or make available for study) fewer topics in greater depth.

AN EXAMPLE: HOMEMAKING

One wonderfully rich topic that rarely appears in the school curriculum is homemaking. The social studies curriculum overflows with nation-making, war-making, and industry-making, but the art of making a home is ignored. The neglect of homemaking and childrearing stems from a long tradition of separating public and private life and assigning greater importance to the former. It is common now to suppose that anyone can make an adequate home; the enterprise supposedly takes no special preparation. As a topic of study, it has been considered intellectually undemanding, one best left to those not intellectually inclined.

But is this true? The historian Theodore Zeldin remarks:

> If home is where one feels comfortable and understood, but still retains one's privacy and mystery, if it is where one both takes care of others and is taken care of, while also having the right to be left alone, and if it is one of the great personal and collective works of art that all humans spend their lives attempting to raise up and keep from falling down, then the art of creating homes, as distinct from building houses, still has a long way to go, and still remains within the province of magic. Instinct and imitation are not enough to make a home. (1994, p. 393)

A unit on homemaking might include history, philosophy, literature, art, music, geography, psychology, and concepts from almost every other discipline. Such a unit might also provide an opportunity for multicultural study. This is clearly an important part of a complete unit on homemaking, but I will consider here only the contemporary Western home—where, indeed, we can see enormous variation in both resources and interests. The home as we know it today is very different from earlier versions. In the Middle Ages, for example, places of shelter often housed businesses, animals, workers, and travelers as well as family, and privacy was rare even in great houses. Comfort as we speak of it now was simply not in the vocabulary. In his history of home (in the Western world), Witold Rybczynski (1986) notes that until the 18th century, "comfort" was associated with consolation, and "comfortable" referred to an adequate level of income. Indeed, he makes the astonishing point that "though the home of 1930 would be familiar to us, it would have been unrecognizable to the citizen of 1885" (p. 220). This is a statement that could introduce study not only of homemaking practices but also of technology, architecture, and changing economic patterns.

Women contributed to the advancement of both comfort and efficiency in homemaking. Catherine Beecher, for example, argued that smaller houses, properly designed, would be both more efficient and more comfortable. She also recommended improved patterns of ventilation. The name of Frederick Winslow Taylor is widely known in the history of the efficiency movement, but somehow the names of Beecher, Christine Frederick, Ellen Richards, Lillian Gilbreth, and Mary Pattison are rarely mentioned (Rybczynski, 1986). Students could be encouraged to investigate some of their work by consulting, among other prominent periodicals, appropriate issues of the *Ladies Home Journal*.

Women in the 19th century pressed for their rights as citizens, but they were not always interested in separating themselves from the care tradition. Often they argued for equal education and voting rights on the grounds that such rights would provide the nation with better homemakers, enlightened mothers, and socially sensitive voters. Of course, this last was sometimes predicated on women's alleged moral superiority. Scarcely anyone would offer such justification today, but it might be interesting for students to gather information and speculate on the roots of the gender gap in contemporary voting patterns on social issues.

A large part of what I am calling the care tradition has centered on homemaking. As Sara Ruddick (1989) has pointed out, the home is where maternal work is done. It is the place "where children are supposed to return when their world turns heartless, where they center themselves in the world they are discovering" (p. 87). It is the place where, in addition to being cared for, children learn to care—to care for other human beings, places, objects, animals, plants, and ideas (Noddings, 1992). In turn, encounters with everything in homes shape the children. What is learned there serves to guide their lives as they wander forth and begin to reshape the world.

Thoughtful educators exploring the simple topic of home might begin to worry that it is far too controversial a topic. Far from being nonintellectual, nonpolitical, and boring, it is loaded with possibilities for radical social action. When we begin to understand how identity is shaped by places (including homes) and how homes become extensions of our own bodies (Casey, 1993), we see clearly how privileged some of us are and how deeply some are deprived. What happens, for example, to the identity of one who is homeless? Here is a wonderful opportunity for students to extend their investigations into the arena of social policy.

RECOGNIZING AND AVOIDING EXPLOITATION

In planning units on homemaking as part of the care tradition, it should not be denied that women have often been exploited as caregivers. Historical study should include the romantic notions associated with Victorian womanhood. A powerful tradition extolled the "angel in the house" while at the same time it exercised enormous effort to keep her there—even forbidding her to read newspapers lest her angelic nature be corrupted. Virginia Woolf's words are important even for today's students. Speaking of that angel, Woolf wrote:

> It was she who used to come between me and my paper when I was writing reviews. It was she who bothered me and wasted my time and so tormented

me that at last I killed her. You who come from a younger generation may not know what I mean by The Angel in the House. . . . She was intensely sympathetic. She was immensely charming. She was utterly unselfish. She excelled in the difficult arts of family life. She sacrificed daily. If there was chicken, she took the leg; if there was a draught, she sat in it—in short she was so constituted that she never had a mind or wish of her own, but preferred to sympathize always with the minds and wishes of others. Above all . . . she was pure. ([reprint]1966, p. 285)

As part of the discussion of women's exploitation, the role of religion should be explored. Even those men who saw clearly that coverture—the system of laws that assimilated married women's interests into those of their husbands—was at odds with liberal ideology often continued to support it. Under these laws, women had no right to control their own property while their husbands lived, could not vote, and were excused for many crimes if those crimes were committed in obedience to husbands. The "laws of God," it was claimed, superseded those of the state and thus justified practices that enforced the subordination of women (Kerber, 1997). Again, one can see that topics related to women's history can be controversial and exciting—perhaps too exciting for today's bland classrooms.

The care tradition can be studied in all its richness and ambiguity in the context of homemaking, nursing, missionary work, settlement houses, campaigns for birth control, child welfare, and peace movements. Such study makes connections with almost every field of human endeavor and encourages a lively concern for the satisfaction of human needs. Students may look on contemporary society and see the importance of the question, Who will care?

THE CONTINUING NEED FOR CARE

As more and more women have claimed their rights to careers and public roles, issues of care have become part of public debate. Clearly, children, the ill, the elderly, and the disabled still need care, and a question arises as to who will provide it. It is easy to respond, the public, or, private, paid caregivers, but neither answer is without difficulties. Even in nations that provide public financial resources for caregiving, complaints are often heard that "nobody cares" (Waerness, 1996). Most human beings, it seems, want care from people who love them, not from paid strangers. Solutions to this problem, if any can be found, will require some creative thought.

Feminists encounter a paradox here. On the one hand, working mothers want low-cost childcare so that their earnings can actually add to family income. On the other hand, low-cost childcare implies low salaries for childcare workers. We can hardly celebrate the liberation of women if some are exploited for the benefit of others. Students can be encouraged to trace the growth of early childhood education, the addition of nurseries to some high schools and workplaces and the gradual rise in subsidies for childcare. They should be invited, too, to analyze the rhetoric surrounding the care of children. Politicians, policymakers, and citizens almost universally speak of children in glowing terms ("our national treasure," "the promise of the future," "our most precious resource"). Paradoxically, many demand proof that early childhood programs produce lasting cognitive gains, and in the absence of such proof want to withdraw funding from the programs; students could address the question, What other benefits might adequate childcare/education programs provide?

No unit on the future of caregiving can be complete without a discussion of personal responsibility. How much responsibility should individuals or families take for the care of their own children, aging parents, or family members who are permanently dependent? This discussion could make use of some economics as well as social theory, and it would be a fine place to introduce students to both classic and contemporary utopias. How have creative thinkers approached these problems? How can social policy today facilitate the personal, private caregiving that so many of us treasure? How might homes, neighborhoods, and cities be designed if the facilitation of caregiving were a criterion of adequacy?

In addition to the somewhat abstract discussion of social utopias and public policy, students need to explore the more concrete and immediate question, Who does the work of caring now? The answer can be found in current sociological studies: Women, even women working regularly outside the home, do the greater amount of housekeeping and childcare. Nancy Fraser (1996) has suggested the need for a universal caregiver model. In most Western societies, certainly in the United States, we have moved to a universal breadwinner model. We now prepare both girls and boys for a future as earners. Both girls and boys now expect to work outside the home, and schooling is clearly organized to meet this expectation. Indeed, one might say with some justification that schools have gone too far in this direction. Bright girls—high achievers—are often advised to abandon traditional female fields and move into math and science. But boys are rarely advised to prepare themselves as caregivers.

A thorough discussion of the future of caregiving will reveal that the male model of dominance is still operating. It is more nearly acceptable now for a woman to be like a man—to enter fields traditionally associated with men—than for a man to be like a woman and become an early childhood educator, nurse, or full-time parent. Worse, as I pointed out above, much of this vitally important work is so denigrated that able women, too, avoid it.

A universal caregiver model would be designed to prepare both girls and boys for the work of caregiving. As both parents become breadwinners, so must both be caregivers, and, of course, caregiving involves much more than watching the kiddies for a few hours. It takes knowledge, energy, and organizational skill to maintain a home that will nurture all of its members. Another possible benefit of a universal caregiver model might be the elevation of caregiving occupations to a status congruent with their value (Gordon, Benner, & Noddings, 1996).

As students study the care tradition and its future, they may ask why homemaking and childrearing are not basic subjects in the school curriculum (Martin, 1985, 1992). This question presents an opportunity to return to the old concept of "separate spheres" (Kerber, 1997) and press further questions about it. Were homemaking and childrearing ever well taught in homes? How many youngsters—even girls—failed to get adequate education for these important tasks? Did their ignorance serve pernicious (if unintended) societal goals? Is such ignorance widespread today? Who gains and who loses from such ignorance?

Finally, in considering the addition of substantial units on caregiving and homemaking to the social studies curriculum, teachers might want to examine the reasons why this has not been done and raise their own critical questions. Are these topics necessarily nonintellectual? Are they well taught at home? Should a sharp line separate public and private life? Should human work be divided into separate spheres? What stands in the way of educating for a universal caregiver model? Just asking these questions amounts to subversive activity. Answering them honestly and creatively may transform our society.

CONCLUSION

In addition to searching for a few women who have participated in public life as equals with men, educators might include the genuine and significant contributions made by women in the care tradition. Inclusion of the care tradition in the social studies curriculum is important for at least two reasons: First, it is a rich tradition that describes the lives and contributions of women; and second, the need for care continues, and study of the care tradition can help girls and boys today learn how to be caregivers, even as both prepare to be breadwinners.

Philosophical and Historical Issues

IN THE NEXT THREE CHAPTERS, I look at the historical roots of character education and the issues in care theory, virtue ethics, and Dewey's pragmatism. Chapter 6 examines the close connection of character education to community and raises the question of whether community can be conceptualized in a way other than that described by traditionalists. It reminds us that community has a dark side—its historical tendency to exclude, and sometimes to harm, those regarded as outsiders.

In Chapter 7, I discuss and critique some of John Dewey's ideas on ethics and education. One of Dewey's great contributions is his analysis of what we might mean by "moral education." In one sense, the expression applies to the enterprise of producing moral people through education. But in a second sense, it points to the morality of the enterprise itself; a moral education is one that is morally justifiable. This second sense is especially important to care theorists because we believe that the conditions of education (its structure, methods, and relationships) are fundamental in the development of moral people. It is also clear in the work discussed here that Dewey was critical of character education for many of the reasons we have already mentioned.

Chapter 8 is a brief and appreciative response to Michael Slote's Distinguished Lecture at the 1999 meeting of the Philosophy of Education Society. In my response, I defend the relational meaning of "caring" against an attempt to fold it into the virtue sense. Virtue ethics and care theory have much in common, but care theory is not a form of virtue ethics. It clearly has features in common with pragmatic moral theory as well, but it is most accurately characterized as belonging to what might be called relational ethics.

Character Education and Community

IN THE LAST DECADE, there has been a considerable increase of interest both in the idea of community and in character education. Indeed, many scholars and policymakers believe that character education must be a function of well-ordered communities. From this perspective, it is insufficient (and perhaps even impossible) for education to produce the disinterested, rational mind long cherished by the liberal tradition. To educate adequately for *character*, a community must stand for something, and it must transmit its values effectively to the young.

THE FOUNDATION OF CHARACTER IN COMMUNITY

Character education as a specific approach to moral education traces its roots to Aristotle (Sichel, 1988). In contrast to views that emphasize reasoning, problem solving, and critical thinking, character education concentrates on the development of virtues. Aristotle devoted most of his *Nicomachean Ethics* to an analysis of the good life and the virtues that it requires and nurtures (Aristotle, 1985). Because the individual is from the start part of a tradition, character education is inextricably joined to community. A strong community defines and exhibits what is meant by the good life; it produces exemplars whose virtues should be emulated.

In contemporary philosophy, Alasdair MacIntyre extols the Aristotelian approach. Each of us, MacIntyre says, is, "whether [one] recognize[s] it or not, one of the bearers of a tradition" (1981, p. 221). From this perspective, each of us is part of a story; we have a role to fill, and certain obligations, rewards, expectations, and virtues accompany that role. Not only are we inevitably part of a story, but we must hear stories to become articulate members of the traditions into which we are born. MacIntyre writes:

> It is through hearing stories about wicked stepmothers, lost children, good but misguided kings, wolves that suckle twin boys, youngest sons who re-

ceive no inheritance but must make their own way in the world and eldest sons who waste their inheritance on riotous living and go into exile to live with the swine, that children learn or mislearn both what a child and what a parent is, what the cast of characters may be in the drama into which they have been born and what the ways of the world are. Deprive children of stories and you leave them unscripted, anxious stutterers in their actions as in their words. Hence, there is no way to give us an understanding of any society, including our own, except through the stock of stories which constitute its initial dramatic resources. (1981, p. 216)

By starting with "wicked stepmothers" and "lost children," MacIntyre violates the recommendations of at least some prominent child psychologists (see, e.g., Bettelheim, 1976), but his point about the centrality of stories is accepted by virtually all character educators and many who do not locate themselves specifically in this school (Coles, 1989). As social beings, we are products of as well as contributors to traditions of behavior. We are not first disengaged, rational mechanisms, and *then* participants in a society; rather, whatever rationality we eventually exhibit is itself a product of the tradition in which we are raised and educated (MacIntyre, 1988; Taylor, 1989).

Stories—biographies, myths, historical accounts, epics, parables—play a central role in establishing identity and in both moral and political education. Michael Oakeshott writes:

And if the understanding of politics I have recommended [a tradition of behavior that includes continuities of conflicts] is not a misunderstanding, there is little doubt about the kind of knowledge and the sort of education which belongs to it. It is knowledge, as profound as we can make it, of our tradition of political behavior. Other knowledge, certainly, is desirable in addition; but this is the knowledge without which we cannot make use of whatever else we may have learned. (1984, p. 232)

Oakeshott puts knowledge about the community and its political traditions first among all forms of knowledge. To convey this knowledge adequately, a community must be concerned not only with the intellectual development of its children but also with their development as moral persons and citizens.

Character education, with its emphasis on stories and tradition, dominated moral education in schools in the United States until around the middle of the 20th century. Early in that century, for example, the Character Development League produced a curriculum designed for use in both homes and schools (White, 1909). Its stated intention was to teach about and develop in children 31 virtues, which, it declared, should culminate in a 32nd integral virtue—character. Particular virtues were assigned to specific grades in school, and teachers were given considerable advice on how to teach each virtue.

This way of approaching moral education was not new with the Character Education League. It was represented earlier in the McGuffey readers (see McClellan, 1999), and, of course, it has long been the dominant mode in religious education. The connection with religion underscores the strong association between character education and community. To be effective, character education must be conducted in a group or society that exhibits widespread agreement on basic values.

The eclipse of character education by cognitive developmentalism in the latter half of the 20th century was caused, at least in part, by a growing sensitivity to the heterogeneity of American society. Many of us began to be aware that Jewish children were uncomfortable with daily recitation of the Lord's Prayer, that nonbelievers might have a sustainable objection to both prayer and Bible-reading in public schools, that, indeed, the population of the United States formed not one community but many. Whatever one's final judgment on this heterogeneity might be—whether one celebrates the recognition or deplores the "disuniting of America" (Schlesinger, 1992)— it must be acknowledged that many earlier abuses and much of the Anglo-Protestant arrogance toward immigrant groups and non-White races was called into question.

In such a climate—one in which a multiplicity of values is acknowledged—cognitive approaches to moral education seem safer and more generous than an approach that requires community homogeneity. Further, cognitive methods are more clearly compatible with the liberal tradition. Instead of attempting to inculcate specific values, advocates of cognitive methods concentrate on the development of moral reasoning. They, too, use stories, but the stories are philosophical fictions designed to trigger critical thinking. If they illustrate a tradition, it is the Enlightenment tradition of Descartes and Kant—one that extols the power of mind and reason. Besides their compatibility with liberal ideology, cognitive methods seem more congruent with the growing emphasis on science and mathematics.

But the shift to cognitive methods raised a host of questions. First, the methods of Kohlberg (1981) and his associates (Power, Higgins, & Kohlberg, 1989)—the most prominent program emphasizing moral reasoning—seem to many to be more suited to research than to teaching. When they are designed for the classroom, teachers need special preparation to use them. The long-accepted expectation that *all* teachers were to be teachers of morals was shaken. Second, the emphasis on reasoning and critical thinking offended many parents and policymakers who prefer a more

Aristotelian emphasis on the inculcation of traditional values. Third, the abstract and theoretical nature of cognitive programs (their "content emptiness") seemed to aggravate a growing sense of alienation in American society. These programs seemed to many to endorse the "purposive-rational action" described by Max Weber as characteristic of modernity (see Bernstein, 1992, p. 54). Such action concentrates on means-ends connections and neglects deliberation and appreciation of ends. The sacred and eternal disappear in a welter of methods and procedures.

These concerns have played a part in reviving interest in community and in traditional values. Conservative philosophers, sociologists, and theologians have been deploring the loss of community throughout the 20th century. For example, in the 1950s, Robert Nisbet wrote:

> Surely the outstanding characteristic of contemporary thought on man and society is the preoccupation with personal alienation and cultural disintegration. . . . The widening concern with insecurity and disintegration is accompanied by a profound regard for the values of status, membership, and community. (1953, p. 3)

More recently, Robert Bellah and his colleagues have raised concern about the loss of biblical and republican traditions. Community spirit, they contend, has been too often sacrificed to individualism and the pursuit of secular and ephemeral forms of self-actualization. Further, real communities are not purposive-rational, loosely linked groups seeking to solve their individual problems. Rather,

> A *community* is a group of people who are socially interdependent, who participate together in discussion and decision making, and who share certain *practices* that both define the community and are nurtured by it. Such a community is not quickly formed. It almost always has a history and so is also a *community of memory*, defined in part by its past and its memory of its past. (Bellah et al., 1985, p. 323)

Strong communities cherish their traditions and see to it that the young are thoroughly acquainted with these traditions. The dependence is two-way. A strong community, according to writers such as MacIntyre, Oakeshott, Bellah, and Nisbet, depends on shared practices, and it is necessary for the production of worthy and acceptable citizens. Moral education—character education—is therefore a central task for a strong community.

The revival of interest in communities has been accompanied by strong philosophical attacks on liberalism. A growing body of critical thought charges that liberalism has overemphasized the autonomy of individuals, perpetuated a myth of the presocial individual, promoted an arrogant universalism (everyone is "just like" us), neglected the role of community, and contributed to the society predicted by Weber—one dominated by a bureaucratic and therapeutic mentality (Weber, 1904–1905/1958).

Whereas liberals favor a society in which procedural fairness ensures that everyone will be able to pursue his or her own legitimate goods (Rawls, 1971), traditionalists and communitarians see such a society as chaotic, even nihilistic. A true society, from this latter perspective, must stand for something; it must establish and discuss the goods it seeks. In this conflict of ideologies, we see a fundamental problem for teachers of morals: How are we to discuss moral issues in productive depth if we do not belong to the same community? How are we to inculcate commonly accepted values in the young if we do not trust one another's motives for doing so? Richard Bernstein, in a sympathetic discussion of Jacques Derrida's ethical position, writes:

> There can be no dialogue, no communication unless beliefs, values, commitments, and even emotions and passions are shared in common. Furthermore, I agree with Gadamer and MacIntyre that dialogic communication presupposes moral virtues—a certain "good will"—at least in the willingness to really listen, to seek to understand what is genuinely other, different, alien, and the courage to risk one's more cherished prejudgments. But too frequently this commonality is not really shared, it is *violently* imposed. A false "we" is projected. (1992, p. 51)

Can the required moral virtues be inculcated without projecting a false "we"? How much commonality is required to do the work of character education?

THE TWO SIDES OF COMMUNITY

Human beings are social animals. We seek not only love and companionship but civic association. The longing for community arises from a deep need to feel a part of something larger than ourselves. The goods we seek in community are captured in a quotation from John Winthrop's "A Model of Christian Charity": "We must delight in each other, make others conditions our own, rejoyce together, mourn together, labor and suffer together, always having before our eyes our community as members of the same body" (quoted in Bellah et al., 1985, p. 28).

However, looking at the same community, James Haught saw a picture at odds with Christian charity:

They created a religious police state where doctrinal deviation could lead to flogging, pillorying, banishment, hanging—or cutting off ears, or boring through the tongue with a hot iron. Preaching Quaker beliefs was a capital offense. Four stubborn Quakers defied this law and were hanged. In the 1690s, fear of witches seized the colony. Twenty alleged witches were killed and 150 imprisoned. (1990, pp. 123–124)

Thus we see in one example the bright side and the dark side of community. In most normal, happy people the longing to belong is balanced by a longing to be free. The theologian Paul Tillich (1952) discussed this balance in some depth and warned against both extremes—the selfishness, alienation, and meaninglessness that result from extreme individualism and the loss of self and fanaticism that arise in totalitarian communities.

Interestingly, both liberals and traditionalists have accused each other of paving the road to totalitarianism. According to the "vacuum" theory expressed by Robert Nisbet, among others, liberalism produces a vacuum of values that, because of the very nature of human beings, must be filled (Nash, 1979). Totalitarian ideologies rush in to fill the vacuum and satisfy the desire to belong. Other conservative critics have seen the form of liberalism that stresses equality (instead of freedom) as the precursor of communism. A third charge, to which we will return because of its present importance, is that liberalism has contributed to the destruction of intermediate groups—families, neighborhoods, religious groups, small charitable organizations, local schools—and thus has undermined the basic units of moral education (Fukuyama, 1995; Glendon, 1991). In its zeal for equality, critics argue, liberalism has placed too much power in the state, which, by its very nature, cannot do the work of civil society.

The charges against liberalism are, however, indirect. In contrast, liberals can point to direct connections between some forms of traditionalism and fascism. For example, despite his plea "for an attitude of piety toward nature, other human beings, and the past," Richard Weaver's (1948) widely read work used language reminiscent of philosophical idealism and fascism. His insistence on distinction, hierarchy, structure, self-discipline, orderliness, and an integrated world picture echoed a message frequently heard in fascist literature (see, e.g., Gentile, 1960).

The sharing and collective orientation advocated by traditionalists can easily be taken to extremes. If it were not for the word "Aryan" in the following and the fact that Adolf Hitler is its author, we might give enthusiastic assent to its basic message:

This will to sacrifice in staking his personal labor and, if necessary, his own life for others, is most powerfully developed in the Aryan. He is greatest, not in his mental capacity *per se*, but in the extent to which he is ready to put all his abilities at the service of the community. With him the instinct of self-preservation has reached the most noble form, because he willingly subjects his own ego to the life of the community and, if the hour should require it, he also sacrifices it. (1939/1925, p. 408)

Thus Tillich was certainly right in warning against the extremes of both individualism and communitarianism. Emphasis on strong communities—the communities of memory praised by Bellah et al.—can lead to the psychological violence feared by Derrida. Ann Russell Mayeaux points to the inadequacy of both communities of memory and communities of terror:

The community of memory engages in self-deception by glamorizing its own past over against the reality of the Other whose speech it pre-empts. The community of terror expunges the past through violence. . . . Thus, it too eradicates the Other's existence. (1993, p. 265)

Mayeaux rejects both the traditionalism of Bellah et al. and the universalism of rules and principles characteristic of liberalism. Instead, she says that we must take personal responsibility for the other. Edith Wyschogrod, too, warns against solutions that are backward-looking:

If liberal theories . . . fail to persuade, it will not do to return nostalgically and uncritically to an older ethos. Nostalgia is amnesia, a wiping out of both the sea changes brought about by recent history and the sins of older communities such as slavery in ancient Greece and the persecution of Jews, Moslems, and heretics by medieval Christianity. This backward thrust is an example of . . . the myth of the tabula rasa and leads to impossible dreams such as Alasdair MacIntyre's hope for the restoration of a monastic ethic or a return to an Aristotelian version of the good life as one governed by the classical virtues. (1990, p. 257)

The postmodern themes suggested by Derrida, Mayeaux, and Wyschogrod prefigure forms of community based on the primacy of the other. We are called upon to listen, to respond to others according to their needs, not according to their membership in a symbolic community or according to "universal" rules that they themselves may reject. It may be that in such communities the virtues to be prized will be relational rather than personal. Relational attributes, such as trust, good cheer, equality, peace, and compatibility, may be more important in such communities than personal virtues, such as courage, honesty, and industry.

However, wherever community is emphasized, character education will be important. As Philip Selznick puts it, "[W]e look to virtue and character as the foundations of morality" (1992, p. 34). Both the actions of individuals and the policies of communities are judged in large part by their consequences for character. Selznick writes: "This is a guide to making rules, and to applying them as well. The question is: What kind of person, institution, or community will result from following a particular course of conduct or from adopting a given rule or policy?" (1992, p. 35).

The difficulty with this sensible position is that someone needs to decide what sort of character we will promote. All responsible parents make such decisions in raising their children, and healthy societies also describe and extol the character they seek to promote. But the enterprise hovers always on the edge of coercion. When we have an ideal in mind, it becomes easy to suppose that people who fail to meet it are, as Isaiah Berlin wrote, "blind or ignorant or corrupt. This renders it easy for me to conceive of myself as coercing others for their own sake, in their, not my, interest" (1969, p. 133).

Selznick would avoid the pitfalls of righteous coercion by embracing a view he calls communitarian liberalism (1992, p. xi). Other sensitive writers also recognize (and would avoid) the dark side of community. John W. Gardner, for example, lists "wholeness incorporating diversity as the first ingredient of today's ideal community" (1991, p. 15). He recognizes how difficult it is to establish this condition—"to prevent the wholeness from smothering diversity—[and] to prevent the diversity from destroying the wholeness" (1991, p. 16; see also Etzioni, 1993). It is especially difficult given that a community by its very nature must have "some core of shared values." Indeed, Gardner says, "of all the ingredients of community this is possibly the most important." And, again, the connection to moral education is explicit:

> The community teaches. If it is healthy it will impart a coherent value system. If it is chaotic or degenerate, lessons will be taught anyway—but not lessons that heal and strengthen. We treasure images of values education in which an older mentor quietly instructs a child in the rules of behavior, but that is a small part of a larger and more turbulent scene. The child absorbs values, good and bad, on the playground, through the media, on the street—everywhere. It is the community and culture that hold the individual in a framework of values. (1991, p. 17)

The difficulties in establishing communities that honor diversity and yet share values (beyond that of diversity) are illustrated in current events. At the level of national politics, where a reasonable example might be set, public figures rarely acknowledge the rightness or wrongness of particular recommendations. Instead, sides are chosen and defended by symbolic identification. Distrust is obvious and pervasive; indeed, it is almost obligatory since lack of it breeds a new form of suspicion, and people are expected to embrace party lines.

In schools, attempts to launch programs of moral education are criticized as much with respect to who suggests them as they are with regard to content. The struggles of the Heartwood curriculum provide a troubling example (Bates, 1995). This curriculum is in the character education tradition; it sets out to illustrate and encourage seven significant virtues, and its stories are collected from a variety of cultures. Thus, in addition to shared values (the seven virtues), it honors cultural diversity. But members of the Christian right have attacked the curriculum because it does not trace the virtues to God as their source. The idea that virtues could arise and be regularly displayed in a secular community is, for these critics, a repugnant one. What can be done in such cases? Even if the schools were to acknowledge (as they are usually willing to do) that some people believe that the virtues are derived only from God, many of these critics would not be satisfied, because they believe that their view is true and thus binding on everyone.

Consider also the continuing arguments over whether and how children should be protected against the media onslaught of sex, profanity, crime, and violence. Many people—perhaps the majority—feel that children should be so protected, but a considerable number argue that this protection should be provided by parents, not by public regulation. In this argument, the liberal emphasis on the freedom of parents to raise their children according to their own conceptions of the good takes top priority. But what is to become of the children whose parents cannot or will not provide such protection? Has the community no responsibility for them?

Many other examples could be given to illustrate the complexity in trying to establish a communitarian liberalism or a liberal communitarianism. Theoretically, the two words—"communitarian" and "liberal"—point to traditions that may be incompatible. One emphasizes communal good; the other, individual goods. In practice, however, if some of the philosophical distinctions are ignored or passed over in favor of listening to and caring for one another, it may be possible to build communities that cherish a core of individual freedom. But the possibility presents enormous problems for schooling. In theory, we can support open dialogue on a nearly full range of topics and opinions, but notice that I have to say "nearly full" because most of us would balk at a "fair hearing" for Nazism or sadism. To complicate matters further, there are groups who are explicitly opposed to the sort of dialogue that seems essential in establishing a community that can care for radically different others and respect ideological diversity. The task will not be an easy one.

A REASONABLE POSITION FOR EDUCATORS

Educators today are especially keen on community building (Sergiovanni, 1994). In part, this great interest is a result of the deterioration of traditional communities. Many educators believe that schools must supply what parents and geographical neighborhoods seem unable to provide—a sense of belonging, of caring for one another, of sharing in a coherent tradition. One of the functions of a community, as we have seen, is to engage in moral education. What role should teachers play in this?

A fundamental premise of traditional education has been that *every* teacher is a teacher of morals (Purpel, 1989). This premise can be construed in two ways: first, that every teacher *should be* a teacher of morals and, second, that every teacher *is*—willingly or not—a teacher of morals. It seems to me that both interpretations are correct. Teachers—even when they deny that they do so—transmit something of moral values (Jackson, Boostrom, & Hansen, 1993), and since this transmission is inevitable, they should seek to do a responsible job of it.

Is it necessary, then, to choose a program of moral education as one might a mathematics or reading curriculum? Must a teacher decide, for example, between character education and cognitive developmentalism? I want to argue in this last section that wise teachers use important ideas from both traditions, and enhance cultural literacy at the same time. For example, stories, judiciously chosen and discussed, can inspire, as character educators claim, set the stage for critical thinking, as cognitivists recommend (Lipman, 1991), and enlarge students' catalog of cultural knowledge (Noddings, 1993).

From this perspective, teachers should not neglect affect and inspiration in favor of detached critical thinking. As we saw in Chapter 4, C. S. Lewis (1955) criticized such attempts strongly, warning that setting aside the emotions would neither provide protection from dogmatism nor satisfy the innate longing most students have for matters that seize the heart. Lewis used as an example the story of the Roman father who taught his son that it is "sweet and seemly" to die for one's country, and he noted that certain advocates of critical thinking have only two choices in their treatment of this story: to debunk it thoroughly or, if they approve of the basic message in the story, to substitute some reasoned argument for young men to submit to military service. Lewis deplores both approaches, for they tend to produce "men without chests"—men who operate with head or guts but no authentic spirit.

However, there is a third choice. One can present a powerful emotional alternative and invite discussion. Thus, I recommended that the story of the Roman father might be followed by Wilfred Owen's "Dulce et Decorum Est" and other poetry highly critical of making war. Further, poetry—that of Rupert Brooke, for example—can also be used to support the message of the Roman father. In such an approach, students encounter the deep passion of opposing positions, and they may come to see that reasonable, decent people often differ dramatically. Besides inspiring and setting the stage for critical discussion, such encounters expand cultural literacy. Students may be encouraged to read Lewis's *The Chronicles of Narnia*. They may be attracted to other powerful poetry and fiction that emerged from the two world wars: the poems of Siegfried Sassoon, Charles Sorley, Joyce Kilmer, and Alan Seeger, as well as those by Owen and Brooke; Remarque's *All Quiet on the Western Front*; or Hemingway's *A Farewell to Arms*. They may learn something of Rome and how this particular story later affected generations of British schoolboys. They may even learn a bit of Latin. Finally, struggling with contradictory ideas thought to be noble and right by opposing sides, they may acquire a tragic sense of life—a sense that even the best critical thinking cannot resolve some of the deepest human dilemmas.

Teachers in all subject areas can use stories effectively, and it is not necessary that the stories always illustrate opposing positions. Sometimes stories can make students aware of continuing social and political problems and assure them that their teachers share the social conscience of a thoughtful community. Mathematics teachers, for example, might use the delightful science fiction story *Flatland* (Abbott, 1952) to further both mathematical and moral interests. *Flatland*, the story of a two-dimensional society, introduces important concepts of dimensionality and relativity, but it is also filled with illustrations of sexism, classism, and religious mysticism. Indeed, mathematics teachers sometimes reject it because of its sexism (even though the sexism is satirical). However, from the perspective taken here, *Flatland*'s sexism, classism, and mysticism give us excellent reasons for discussing such matters in mathematics classes. Imagine a society in which all males are polygons, and class status depends on the number of one's sides. Isosceles triangles are the working poor, so to speak, and those polygons with so many sides that they are almost indistinguishable from circles are the priests at the top of the social hierarchy. Every father in Flatland hopes that his sons will have more sides than he has. What of women? In this highly stratified society, women are, through all generations, mere line segments. They are, no matter the status of their husbands, essentially nonpersons.

In addition to classism and sexism, *Flatland* introduces a good bit of mysticism. The narrator of the story, an upstanding square, is visited by a three-dimensional entity. Of course, no one believes him, and he finishes his tale in prison. He is regarded as either mad or subversive but definitely dangerous to his community. In the mystical tradition, he longs for another visitation, something to affirm what he knows really happened. But how can one explain a third dimension to people living in two-dimensional space? How would we describe a four-dimensional entity to our peers?

Stories like *Flatland* not only help to build community through shared ideas and conversation, but they provide an opportunity to criticize community and develop some of the cautionary ideas discussed earlier. Communities often fail to accept dissenting or unusual ideas. They demand conformity and punish dissent. They may also establish rigid rules for belonging and use the rules to exclude people whose symbolic affiliations preclude their acceptance of the rules. Discussion of such issues is vital if we are to avoid the dark side of community.

Teachers prepared with a repertoire of inspiring stories probably also have an advantage in keeping their students' attention. By acknowledging a wide variety of legitimate interests in their students, such teachers demonstrate their own commitment to a way of educating that is moral in its procedures as well as its content.

Stories are not the only feature of moral education that is compatible with both character education and cognitive approaches. We could talk about the role of conversation in all its forms—from philosophical argumentation to everyday conversation. We could profitably discuss practice—how to demonstrate moral behavior in our teaching and how to provide students with opportunities to care for one another. Many ideas from each school of thought might be examined carefully to see whether they can be taken up or honestly adapted by the other. I have concentrated here on stories because their use seems so obviously acceptable to both groups.

I'll finish with a question for further investigation. Why are teachers so poorly prepared to draw on stories in their disciplinary instruction? There may be a wide and dangerous gap between the narrow expertise characteristic of today's liberal studies and the equally narrow expertise of professional schools. Too often there is little of the truly liberal in the content of liberal studies (Wilshire, 1990) and not much content in professional studies. Disciplines traditionally included in the liberal arts have become, for the most part, highly specialized centers of expertise. Few professors in these disciplines address the questions that were once thought to be central to liberal studies: How should I live? What kind of life is worth living? How do I find meaning in life? (Naylor, Willimon, & Naylor, 1994). Education schools and departments also fail to address these questions and concentrate on pedagogy, classroom management, school structure, and related topics. The sort of knowledge that relates subject matter and teaching itself to the great questions of life seems to have fallen into a chasm. If such a gap does in fact exist, we need to fill it in so that teachers will be prepared to do the work of moral education.

Thoughts on Dewey's "Ethical Principles Underlying Education"

In "Ethical Principles Underlying Education," Dewey (1897/1972) introduces many topics that he will develop more fully in later works: the child as an organic whole, the integral quality of ethics in life and in schools, the inclusive nature of citizenship, the need for increasing practice in accepting responsibility, the proper role of school subjects in education, the dynamic and practical nature of intelligence, the lamentable separation of intellectual and moral training, the mistaken notion that the individual and the community are necessarily in conflict, and many others. Indeed, it would be difficult to summarize this article without simply reproducing it. Instead, I will concentrate on two main themes, how Dewey develops them, and a difficulty that seems to be inherent in Dewey's moral theory.

When Dewey speaks of ethics in education, he works with two aspects, or themes: First, he lays down guidelines for the ethical *conduct* of education; second, he discusses what might be called the ethical *product*—moral citizens. It is in this second aspect that I find a troubling omission, but let's start with the first.

THE ETHICAL CONDUCT OF EDUCATION

Dewey starts his essay by declaring that there "cannot be two sets of ethical principles . . . one for life in the school, and the other for life outside of school" (p. 54).[1] Already, some readers will be prepared to challenge him. The school, some will argue, is a specialized institution designed to work with the immature. Surely, as John Stuart Mill (1859/1993) acknowledged with respect to the principles of liberalism, one cannot responsibly use the same ethical principles with children as with adults. But Dewey insists, "As conduct is one, the principles of conduct are one also" (p. 54).

Dewey seeks to direct attention to a level of principle at which his basic postulate holds. Of course, children must be treated differently from adults, but this different treatment is properly based on differences of experience. The *principles* of conduct are the same for children and adults, inside and outside school. He warns against making a theoretical leap from principles to the differences in conduct that inevitably show up "at the point of application." Of course, teaching a five-year-old is different from teaching a graduate student; nursing is different from crime prevention, and so on, but these differences should not obscure fundamental similarities at the level of principle.

Dewey does not define "conduct" but launches immediately into a discussion of its integral character and the principles governing it. We may assume, however, that he means by "conduct" all the purposeful doings in which human beings engage.

For the sake of analysis, Dewey takes up the two aspects of conduct separately: the *what* of conduct ("its actual filling") and the *how* ("ways, means, and processes"). He puts it this way:

> The psychological view of conduct has to do, then, with the question of agency, of how the individual operates; the social, with what the individual does and needs to do, considered from the standpoint of his membership in a whole which is larger than himself. (p. 56)

Dewey uses the example of a man starting a business of manufacturing cloth to show that the needs of society establish the manufacturer's ends. Society's needs and demands fix "the meaning and value of what he does." But the individual must find the ways and means to satisfy these social needs. In a paragraph that presages work he will do later on the shifting nature of means and ends, he shows how the manufacturer's search for means will establish new ends and how ends will become means to still other ends. Then he writes:

> I think this parallelism may be applied to moral conduct without the change of a single principle. It is not the mere individual as an individual who makes the final demand for moral action, who establishes the final end, or furnishes the final standards of worth. It is the constitution and development of the larger life into which he enters which settles these things. But when we come to the question of how the individual is to meet the moral demands, of how he is to realize the values within himself, the question is one which concerns the individual as an agent. Hence it must be answered in psychological terms. (p. 57)

Here Dewey has set up a problem that many of us believe he never addressed adequately. Is the society as it is the sole determiner of what is moral? We know that Dewey will insist on locating the moral within the social (not in God, a special faculty, or established authority), but we also know that he wants education to move beyond socialization—indeed, that he wants the workings of intelligence to improve society. Will "the social" inevitably cast up criteria that are reliably moral, or must we mean by "moral" whatever the social group establishes as normative? I will return to this very important question in the last section.

In the meantime, it is easy to see why social processes are so vital in Dewey's program. *If* the social processes are of a certain sort, then in fact we can count on the group to formulate norms that would be widely regarded as moral. For Dewey, ways and means and ends and outcomes form a whole. We cannot use dictatorial means to educate democratic citizens; we cannot expect students to master skills if the skills are taught outside the domain of application; we cannot effectively teach children who are "organic wholes" as though they were mere collections of attributes or "faculties."

If we want to conduct education ethically, then, we must consider what we do from both social and psychological perspectives. The child is both an individual (an organic whole) and a member of a certain kind of society. Dewey acknowledges the school's moral responsibility to the society in strong terms; the school exercises "a certain specific function in maintaining the life and advancing the welfare of society." Further, "the educational system which does not recognize this fact as entailing upon it an ethical responsibility is derelict and a defaulter" (p. 58).

Having said this, Dewey then launches into the discussion that has endeared him to generations of educators. He notes that citizenship has been construed too narrowly, that the child is to be not only a voter but "a member of a family, himself responsible . . . in turn, for rearing and training of future children, and thus maintaining the continuity of society" (p. 58). He will be a worker, a member of a local community, a contributor to the "decencies and graces of civilization." Thus Dewey warns against the isolation of formal citizenship from "the whole system of relations with which it is actually interwoven" (p. 59).

Dewey notes also that children in the United States are to be educated for *democratic* citizenship, which requires powers of self-direction, administration, and responsibility. Training in mere obedience is insufficient. Further, life in the industrial United States is dynamic, constantly changing. Therefore, the child must be educated so that "he may take charge of himself; may not only adapt himself to the changes which are going on, but have power to shape and direct those changes" (p. 60).

Again, even as we admire and accept most of Dewey's advice on the conduct of education, we may worry about the criteria children will use to "shape and direct" change. We know they must be social, but can the social be relied upon to shape itself? A great deal hangs on Dewey's conception of "social"; its importance is revealed in the following passage:

> We get no moral ideals, no moral standards for school life excepting as we so interpret in social terms. To understand what the school is actually doing, to discover defects in its practice, and to form plans for its progress means to have a clear conception of what society requires and of the relation of the school to these requirements. (p. 61)

But since people disagree on what society requires, on the relation of school to these requirements, and even on what is meant by "social," how are we to proceed? Dewey answers this question indirectly with a lifetime of work. The social itself is to be worked out in interaction, in a commitment to continued communication and inquiry. Social life is not fixed. Whatever its form, however, if it is committed to an ideal of continued inquiry, its workings must be reflected in the society's schools: "The school cannot be a preparation for social life excepting as it reproduces, within itself, the typical conditions of social life" (pp. 61–62). Again, "the only way to prepare for social life is to engage in social life" (p. 62).

With this principle in mind, Dewey pokes fun at those who would teach children to swim outside of the water, to write checks and balance budgets when they have no checking accounts or incomes, to memorize legislative structures and forms when they have no say in what is legislated. He asks educators to consider which of the habits we try so hard to inculcate in schools are really useful for life and which are only required because of the artificial workings of schools.

These are wonderful pages, filled with ideas familiar to all Dewey readers from others of his works, pages that describe the child's interests in construction, inquiry, creative expression, and communication; the connection between purposes and outcomes; the need to encourage intrinsic interests; the blend of intellectual and manual in "manual" training; the indissociable connection between the intellectual and the moral.

Dewey devotes several pages to a discussion of the content and form of the school curriculum. "The contention is that a study is to be considered as bringing the child to realize the social scene of action; that when thus considered it gives a criterion for the selection of material and for the judgment of value" (p. 67). The pages that follow contain ideas elaborated in *The School and Society* (1900/1990), *The Child and the Curriculum* (1902/1990), *Democracy and Education* (1916), and finally *Experience and Education* (1938/1963). All subjects are to be taught as contributions to social life. They must be connected at one end to the child's experience and at the other to the social life in which the child will take part.

There can be no better summary of this part of the discussion than Dewey's own:

> I sum up, then, this part of the discussion by asking your attention to the moral trinity of the school. The demand is for social intelligence, social power, and social interests. Our resources are (1) the life of the school as a social institution in itself; (2) methods of learning and of doing work; and (3) the school studies or curriculum. In so far as the school represents, in its own spirit, a genuine community life; in so far as what are called school discipline, government, order, etc., are the expressions of this inherent social spirit; in so far as the methods used are those which appeal to the active and constructive powers, permitting the child to give out, and thus to serve; in so far as the curriculum is so selected and organized as to provide the material for affording the child a consciousness of the world in which he has to play a part, and the relations he has to meet; in so far as these ends are met, the school is organized on an ethical basis. (pp. 75–76)

Moral life is grounded in social life, but what justifies the form of social life that Dewey will later develop and defend? Surely, some of the criteria for a defensible social life are moral in a sense that transcends a particular form of social life. Dewey does not give us much help here, and we may rightly fear that his "moral trinity" might be applied as effectively in morally questionable settings as in those Dewey prefers.

THE ETHICAL PRODUCT OF EDUCATION

Dewey urges us not only to conduct education ethically but also to work toward the education of moral citizens, and his discussion of moral education is important even today. One might expect him to discuss moral education as part of the psychological aspect of ethical principles. But, true to his insistence that the moral is social, he first discusses it as part of the social aspect of education and, particularly, as one of the contributions made by the appropriate teaching of history. He argues gently against what we today call character education:

> What the normal child continuously needs is not so much isolated moral lessons instilling in him the importance of truthfulness and honesty, or the beneficial results that follow from some particular act of patriotism, etc. It is the formation of habits of social imagination and conception. (p. 72)

Later in the same paragraph, he reveals what some would regard as faith in humanity and others might rightly regard as naiveté:

> The evils of the present industrial and political situation, on the ethical side, are not due so much to actual perverseness on the part of individuals concerned, nor in mere ignorance of what constitutes the ordinary virtues (such as honesty, industry, purity, etc.) as to inability to appreciate the social environment in which we live. It is tremendously complex and confused. (pp. 72–73)

Even in his later works (those written between 1925 and 1953), Dewey seemed to hold this view—that perverse and mean acts are usually the result of failure to think, not of thinking toward wicked ends. He says, for example:

> And if we take the case of a person commonly considered immoral, we know that he does not take the trouble of justifying his acts, even criminal ones; he makes no effort, to use the psychoanalysts' term, to "rationalize" them. (quoted in Gouinlock, 1994, p. 157)

Surely Dewey is wrong on this. Just recently I listened to teenagers on the Jersey shore rationalize their habit of stealing: "It's okay to steal from jerks but not from people like us." (One boy turned down an opportunity to steal when he learned that the intended victim was a surfer—presumably not a "jerk.") "It's okay to steal if you really need the money, but you shouldn't take more than you need." "It's okay to steal from big stores but not from little ones or from individuals who don't have much." Further, news reports are filled with the rationalizations of national and local officials who have chosen the expedient over the moral. The skillful analysis of means and ends does not necessarily culminate in the morally good. If people did not believe this earlier, the events of the 20th century should have convinced us that neither critical thinking nor the usual forms of social interaction will prevent evil acts.

Moreover, powerful thinking, even in the service of commonly accepted moral goods, will not always bring us out in the same place. This last Dewey understood—that moral matters are so complex that no easy solutions are forthcoming. But he still believed that critical and constructive action (guided by similar thought) is our main hope. "Most people are left at the mercy of tradition, impulse, or the appeals of those who have special and class interests to serve," he remarks, and the remedy is the sort of education that "develops that power of observation, analysis, and inference with respect to what makes up a social situation and the agencies through which it is modified" (p. 73). He did not seem to understand that some people *choose* after careful thought, to follow tradition or special interests even when neither works toward the most intelligent and generous social life.

Dewey notes that "it is a commonplace" to regard character development as the ultimate end of schooling, but, he contends, the concept of character used by educators remains unclear. True to his dynamic and interactional perspective, he refers to character "as a piece of running, physical machinery" (p. 78). Character, as the "power of social agency," has three constituents: force or energy, judgment, and emotional responsiveness. Dewey discusses each of these in turn.

Force (energy, will) is necessary to carry out good intentions, which are in themselves empty— "wishy-washy." A person of character must have "initiative, insistence, persistence, courage and industry"; he or she "must have the power to stand up and count for something in the actual conflicts of life" (p. 79). Dewey goes on to note that people are born with different capacities in this respect. It is one function of education to discover what these capacities are and to develop them as far as possible. It is clear from the paragraph on force and from his later writings that Dewey favored an appropriate environment for every child—one that would challenge forth but not overwhelm very different innate capacities.

But force of character must be directed by sound judgment. "Judgment is ideas directed with reference to the accomplishment of ends," and "good judgment is a sense of respective or proportionate values" (p. 79). The development of judgment involves more than knowledge or information; it requires constant practice, encouragement, and astute guidance. Educators must attend to the instincts and impulses of students and guide them into constructive activities. Neither coercion nor permissiveness will promote the development of judgment. With permissiveness, Dewey says, we simply spoil the child; with coercion, we risk producing unintelligent and insensitive adults.

I see that risk illustrated in the story, mentioned earlier, that George Orwell tells of his early school years at "Crossgates." Physical abuse was the standard pedagogy at Crossgates, and it was effective in getting small boys to learn Latin, English grammar, and the dates of historical events. No judgment was required on the part of students. Indeed, the exercise of judgment would have been regarded as impudence. The results were fear, hatred, despair, and rote learning that would have produced fine scores on standardized tests. Referring to the headmaster, Sim, and his wife, Bingo, Orwell writes. "I hated Bingo and Sim, with a sort of shamefaced, remorseful hatred, but it did not occur to me to doubt their judgment" (1956, p. 431). Having been caned once for bedwetting and again, harder, for confiding that the first "didn't hurt," young George learned the "abiding lesson" of his boyhood: "that I was in a world where it was *not possible* for me to be good. . . . Life was more terrible, and I was more wicked, than I had imagined" (1946/1981, p. 5).

Dewey encourages educators to provide a social environment in which it *is* possible for children to be good and in which they will learn to exercise sound judgment so that the larger society to which they will belong will become still better through their wise participation. In reading Dewey, one must remember that he was reacting, at least in part, to the widespread use of physical and psychological coercion, a coercion still firmly in place when Orwell went to school almost two decades later.

Encouraging the development of judgment in students might in fact discourage rote learning (and thus reduce some test scores), but Dewey was not interested in the mere acquisition of information. He was concerned with its intelligent application. Therefore, students were to be involved intelligently from start to finish in the work they undertook in school: in the construction of objectives, in the choice of means, in evaluating the results, in generalizing for future learning.

However, even force directed by judgment is insufficient for good character. Dewey insisted also on "a delicate personal responsiveness—there must be an emotional reaction" (p. 80). He says that "it is difficult to put this quality into words," but he draws our attention to the kind of sensitivity we all prefer to live with, characterized "by tact, by instinctive recognition of the claims of others, by skill in adjusting" (p. 80).

Although Dewey clearly favored and wanted to promote a form of character that would be sensitive and responsive to the needs of others, he never included such a criterion in his formal definitions. We can well imagine a character that fits his three criteria—force, judgment, and emotional reaction—and is still directed toward horrendous acts. We can no longer imagine such a character when we see how Dewey fills out the description of each criterion, but we may well wonder why he did not pause to discuss the inadequacy of the criteria as originally stated. Again, I suspect he saw no inadequacy. His consuming faith in a process that calls into play energy, judgment, and feeling led him to overlook the possibility that all three working together could nevertheless culminate in moral atrocities.

Many of us wish Dewey had said more about emotional responsiveness. He does say quite a bit about it in connection with intellectual development but less in connection with moral development. (His refusal to separate the intellectual and the moral may be one reason for his brevity here.) In this essay, he includes only a brief paragraph toward the end on the development of "susceptibility and responsiveness." It is worth quoting in full because the point at issue is so important today:

> The informal, social side of education, the aesthetic environment and influences, are all-important here. In so far as all the work is laid out in regular and formulated ways, in so far as there are lacking opportunities for casual

and free social intercourse between the pupils, and between the pupils and the teacher, this side of the child's nature is either being starved or else left to find haphazard expression along more or less secret channels. When the school system under plea of the practical (meaning by the practical the narrowly utilitarian) confines the child to the three R's and the formal studies connected with them, and shuts him out from the vital sources of literature and history, and deprives him of his right to contact with what is best in architecture, music, sculpture and picture, it is hopeless to expect any definite results with respect to the training of this integral element in character. (p. 82)

But much more needs to be said about the education of sensibility. Traditional education, for all its faults, often attended meticulously to the cultivation of feelings, particularly those involved in patriotism and religion. Stories, music, and art were chosen specifically to induce feelings endorsed by the society (as defined by those in power). For at least a decade after Dewey's essay, educators were still concentrating heavily on the education of character through literature and the arts (White, 1909). One might plausibly argue that Dewey's recommendations were often interpreted as attempts to shift the emphasis from traditional devotion to critical thinking.

By the 1950s critics were beginning to worry that schools had gone too far in their emphasis on critical thinking. As discussed earlier, C. S. Lewis (1955) criticized such approaches strongly, warning that setting aside the emotions would neither provide protection from dogmatism nor satisfy the innate longing most students have for matters that seize the heart.

Clearly, Dewey would agree with this warning, but one is hard put to demonstrate his concern in his moral writings. In his *Ethics*, "emotion" does not even appear in the index, and only a few pages are listed for "Kant on feelings." Similarly, in his other writings on moral philosophy and moral education, little attention is given to a criterion he names here as central. He seems to have had an almost Dickensian revulsion toward do-goodism, and probably the hypocrisy that accompanied so much of the romantic period disgusted him as well. He insists on a practical approach to moral life, counseling that we need "a genuine, not merely nominal faith in the existence of moral principles which are capable of effective application" (p. 82). That he is reacting against hypocrisy is clear when he writes:

We believe in moral laws and rules, to be sure, but they are in the air. They are something set off by themselves. They are so *very* "moral" that there is no working contact between them and the average affairs of everyday life. What we need is to have these moral principles brought down to the ground through their statement in social and in psychological terms. (p. 83)

We may agree wholeheartedly with Dewey that moral matters pervade ordinary life and are practical, that they call for courage (or "force") and judgment. But Dewey may be wrong in refusing to recognize the moral as a domain to be discussed in its own right. Consider an analogy. We might, at an appropriate level of abstraction, claim that the same sort of thinking is required for engineering as for cooking (and for everything else, according to Dewey). But surely we need to give much attention to what Dewey calls the "point of application." There are standards and guidelines in engineering that are particular to engineering as a field and bear little resemblance to those in cooking. In a domain as central to human life as morality, we need to say much more than Dewey does about the specific criteria by which we make *moral* judgments.

I agree with Dewey that the line between the moral and the nonmoral has been drawn much too rigidly, but it may be even more important to discuss specifically moral criteria as we expand the domain. Again, in several later works, Dewey insists that the virtues involved in good character are not fixed, nor are they best construed as inner possessions of individuals. They are effective habits called forth in particular situations, and they cannot be usefully discussed in isolation, "but rather in interpenetration" (Rice, 1996, p. 277). Indeed, Dewey (1930) later identified this interpenetration of habits with character.

Dewey has told us much more about the ethical conduct of education than about the ethical product. Like so many liberals of both yesterday and today, he puts enormous faith in right procedures. But will these procedures produce recognizable moral goods? That question still haunts us.

BEYOND DEWEY? SOME THOUGHTS

In "Ethical Principles" and many later works, Dewey made two important contributions to moral thought: First, he reminded us that there is a moral aspect of almost everything we do, and second, he showed how the methods common to science could be used effectively in the moral domain. Critics who want to delimit the moral domain, especially in education, sometimes ask, What's moral about math teaching? Dewey argued persuasively that, beyond the fair and humane treatment of students as persons, even the selection of content has a moral aspect: Is the material connected to the students' experience? Will it contribute to their growth? Does it have demonstrable social worth? These are questions with obvious moral implications.

The second contribution, his method, has incurred more criticism. On the positive side, Dewey has liberated us from fixed principles and external authority. He has encouraged us to solve moral problems as we would any others—by thinking through all likely scenarios to their likely consequences. The method is powerful. In the *Ethics*, he describes it as dramatic rehearsal:

> Deliberation is actually an imaginative rehearsal of various courses of conduct. We give way, *in our mind*, to some impulse; we try, *in our mind*, some plan. Following its career through various steps, we find ourselves in imagination in the presence of the consequences that would follow; and as we then like and approve, or dislike and disapprove, these consequences, we find the original impulse or plan good or bad. (Dewey & Tufts, 1908/1978, p. 293)

Dewey points out that a mental trial is "retrievable." We need not enact it. Thus we are led to think through our options and behave responsibly in the sense that we must be willing, in case we *do* enact the plan, to take responsibility for the consequences that we have foreseen. But what induces the approval or disapproval Dewey foresees? Are there consequences we *should* approve or disapprove? And is an act to be judged moral simply because the actor accepts responsibility for it? These are questions, it seems to me, that Dewey never answered adequately. We are still troubled by the need for specifically moral criteria. Scattered throughout his work, we find descriptions of desirable and undesirable behaviors, of generous or niggardly attitudes, but we never find these tied to his method in a way that guides either the decisionmaker or an observer who may pass judgment on the decision.

Approval, for Dewey, must be clearly connected to the welfare of both society and the individual who gives or withholds approval. But what if I approve, for example, of the vision of a society free of ethnic minorities? What if I am willing to take responsibility for massive shifts in population so that like may live with like? If I assess the immediate consequences and see a certain amount of misery but, in contrast, see an eventual future that is peaceful and prosperous, do those long-range consequences outweigh the short-term miseries? Further, if most of the substantial citizens in the society agree with me, is it moral to go ahead with such a plan?

Dewey would likely respond by saying that in a democracy, all those who have a stake in the outcome must share in deliberation. But how much weight should be given to objections? Dewey cannot pronounce certain acts absolutely wrong, nor will he settle for the mere calculation of collective goods and harms. If we do not arrive at consensus through acceptable means of persuasion, what are we do to?

Dewey acknowledges that we may reasonably use Aristotle's "good man" test in our deliberations. What would the best person we know do in such a situation? Asking such a question may indeed be useful, but for Dewey, it cannot be conclusive:

> And while this method cannot supply the standard of their own judgment, cannot determine the right or wrong for their own situations, it helps emancipate judgment from selfish partialities, and it facilitates a freer and more flexible play of imagination . . . (Dewey & Tufts, 1908/1978, p. 294)

But what if we consciously or unconsciously choose a model that reinforces our own initial judgment? My choice of a "good person" may be, from an objective view, a bad choice. It is not clear how the identification of a good person can serve to emancipate judgment and make it more flexible. It might conceivably have the opposite effect.

It is entirely possible to discuss harm, pain, and care in a naturalistic moral philosophy. It is not Dewey's naturalism that stands in the way. Further, the criteria of judgment need not be stated as rigid or absolute principles, but they must acknowledge certain universals in the human condition. They can be stated as questions to which certain kinds of answers are preferred: Will this cause harm or unnecessary pain? (If so, try to avoid doing it.) Does this being need some form of care from me? (What can I reasonably do, given the demands currently existing in my network of care?) At least these questions must be asked, and it is implied in their asking that as we use Dewey's method of deliberation, we will approve or disapprove likely consequences on the basis of avoiding harm and pain and providing care where it is needed. These criteria are based on factors—avoiding pain and requiring care—that are actually universal in the human condition. As such, the criteria are themselves very nearly absolute. Reading his life, rather than his words, I believe Dewey would agree.

NOTE

1. Unless otherwise noted, parenthetical page numbers refer to "Ethical Principles Underlying Education" (Dewey, 1897/1972).

Two Concepts of Caring

IN THE LAST CHAPTER, I discussed Dewey's two senses of "moral educa-tion" and pointed out that for Dewey, the first sense—moral education as education that can be morally justified—is of fundamental importance. An emphasis on the social relationships in classrooms, students' interest in the subject matter to be studied, and the connections between classroom life and that of the larger world provides the foundation for our attempts to produce moral people. As educators, we must make it both possible and desirable for students to be good. This imperative implies special consid-eration of the caring relations that support the development of virtues.

In his thoughtful paper "Caring Versus the Philosophers," Michael Slote (2000) makes several important comments supportive of caring as a moral orientation. Here I want to say something about the justice/care debate and a little about the claim that caring has its own answer to deon-tology on the killing/letting die issue. Then I will concentrate on the only issue that clearly separates us—whether to emphasize care as a virtue or as a relation.

It may well be that Slote is right when he says that care theorists have backed off too quickly in acknowledging the need for justice as a neces-sary supplement to care. But backing off is good for the philosophical soul. We learn, and sometimes we gather greater strength, in partial retreat. I think now that my own error was in giving too little attention to "caring about." In more recent work (Noddings, 2002), I explore the need to ana-lyze "caring about" in much more detail. Earlier, in *Caring,* I had written:

> I have brushed aside "caring about" and, I believe, properly so. It is too easy. I can "care about" the starving children of Cambodia, send five dollars to hunger relief, and feel somewhat satisfied. I do not even know if my money went for food, or guns, or a new Cadillac for some politician. This is a poor second-cousin to caring. "Caring about" always involves a certain benign neglect. One is attentive just so far. One assents with just so much enthusi-asm. One acknowledges. One affirms. One contributes five dollars and goes on to other things. (Noddings, 1984, p. 112)

I still believe that the basic distinction between "caring for" and "caring about" is right, and at the time my intention was to emphasize the special nature of "caring for." "Caring about" can deteriorate to political self-righteousness and to forms of intervention that do more harm than good. (Think here of Mrs. Jellyby and other insufferable characters from the novels of Charles Dickens.) But "caring about" may be the foundation of justice. It is physically impossible for any one of us to "care for" all of humanity—strangers who have not addressed us directly or those unknown others at a great distance. Still, when we have acquired the attitude of care, we feel impelled to do something for any people who are suffering. "Caring about" becomes a sense of justice; it is important, and often it is the only form of caring available to us. However, I see it as morally important because it is instrumental in establishing the conditions under which "caring for" can flourish. This insistence on completion in the other is central to care theory, and it suggests a reason for not giving way on the present emphasis on relation.

The balance discussed by Slote (between caring inside and outside the inner circle) is clearly important in individual lives. The Mrs. Jellybys of the world are so busy "caring about" faraway and unknown others that they do not even see the misery or joy right in front of them. They fail almost entirely to care for those close to them. Their failure is even more shocking when we see that their "caring about" does not eventuate in "caring for." The misery of the faraway recipients of their care is increased by justified resentment. But clearly there is something to worry about in the other extreme as well—those who care only for their own. Here, too, at its worst, caring is warped into something pathological, and the recipients of such care may become selfish and insensitive. Thus, practically, balance is important. But, theoretically, it is vital to place "caring for" over "caring about." This is an inversion of Kantian ethics that recognizes the centrality of meeting others in caring relations and the futility of trying to solve moral problems completely and universally in abstract and codified schemes.

On this first point, then, I think Slote and I are in substantial agreement. As a virtue theorist, he puts (perhaps) more emphasis on a balance between the two forms of caring. I, as an advocate of a thoroughly relational approach, put greater emphasis on the carer's responsibility to follow through—to see whether his or her "caring about" results in "caring for." A balance may depend as much on available resources, aesthetic sensibilities, and intellectual virtues as it does on moral virtue. Following through insists on the importance of the response triggered in the cared-for.

I think Slote is clearly right when he argues that caring "has its own resources for disallowing killing as a means to saving . . . lives"—even other deeply loved lives. In *Caring*, I wrote that a carer faced with this sort of dilemma might be tempted to sacrifice someone for the sake of several others:

> My eye falls on A. He is sick and probably will not live through the arduous trip home. He is unmarried. He will not struggle. Perhaps I can avoid his eyes. But as I reach toward him, I feel the life, and fear, and trust, and hope, and whatever else is emanating from him. My long practice in receiving holds me back. (Noddings, 1984, p. 106)

But this is a description of both moral strength and human tragedy. It is not a prescription, not a principle to be consulted. It might even be described, alternatively, as moral weakness or just plain "lack of guts." Human beings have been forced into such horrible decisions (think here of *Sophie's Choice*), and any ethical theory that condemns or praises one choice or another lacks a necessary compassion. Who would dare to sit in judgment on persons in such predicaments? Caring condemns the villains and the conditions that force such choices on human sufferers, but it folds protective arms about those tragic figures who have had to make such forced choices.

Now we come to a matter of substantive disagreement. Should care assume a place of respectability in the accepted category of virtue ethics? Although care theorists have much in common with virtue ethicists, the answer must be a respectful no. That there is considerable overlap and that there is much to be gained in debate cannot be denied, but emphasis on the relational meaning of care should not be abandoned.

When I started work on caring, I was not aware of the two meanings of caring—one referring to a virtue, the other to a special attribute of relations. Astonishingly, I was not even aware of the gender aspects of the topic. It was Bill Pinar, at a meeting of the John Dewey Society in Dallas, 1980, who pointed this out to me. "I hope you don't mind," he said, and that gentle comment launched me into feminist studies, a field totally new to me. Much more recently, through talks with Larry Blum and the writings of Slote, I have become aware of the virtue/relation distinction. Both concepts are useful, but care theory itself makes its special contribution through the relational sense.

We do, of course, use the virtue sense regularly. We speak of a caring parent, a caring teacher, a caring physician. I am not suggesting that we abandon this language, but I think it is not the best starting point. If we take the caring relation as a basic good, then all efforts to establish, maintain, or enhance such relations have moral worth. Slote counsels that it seems odd to credit those who accept our care with moral points of some kind. After all, we are the ones putting forth the moral effort. But acknowledgment of the contribution of recipients of care may be the very heart of care theory. It recognizes moral interdependence. There is nothing in traditional moral theory that will permit us to recognize anything distinctively moral about the responsive infant's contribution to the parent-child caring relation, and in fact we need not talk this way. Without giving the kind of credit we usually reserve for moral agents, we can still acknowledge that the contribution to moral life is real. So are the contributions of responsive students to the teacher-student relation and of the responsive patient to the physician-patient relation. Care theory tries to capture and describe these contributions.

Slote is right to say that carers should not be blamed for every breakdown in caring relations. Indeed, care theorists agree fully. A carer may get full moral credit (in the virtue sense) for heroic efforts at care, and yet that same carer may have to acknowledge that the relation is not one of caring. The fault may lie with the cared-for or with the situation in which the relation is located. In schools today, for example, we hear many students complain that "nobody cares." When we talk with teachers in the same schools, we may be convinced that these teachers do care and care deeply in the virtue sense. But something has gone badly wrong. People who are trying to care and people who want care have been unable to form caring relations. We cannot just say, Well, we cared. We have to admit a failure (a form of no-fault failure, perhaps) and analyze the situation that makes caring so difficult.

I started out thinking of care as a primary, even as a universal human attribute. After a discussion with Jim Gibbs, a Stanford anthropologist, I was convinced that caring may not be universal. What is universal, Gibbs said, is the desire to be cared for, the desire for caring relations. There is nothing moral about that desire in itself. But its universality makes it reasonable to posit the caring relation as a primary good. Manifestations of the desire to be cared for range from the absolute need of infancy to the aloof desire to be treated with respect that is so characteristic of mature persons in individualistic cultures. The manifestations differ over cultures, times, and individuals. But this relation is everywhere taken as a basic good.

The desire to be cared for calls forth in most well-cared-for people a moral response, and admitting that gives considerable weight to Slote's recommendation that caring be made morally fundamental. But caring has a point, namely, to respond to a cared-for. That response cannot always satisfy an expressed desire (indeed, there are times when it should not do so), but it should always try to maintain the relation in which address and response can be continued or picked up after a period of silence ("leaving alone") in which the relation is empty of encounter. Further, maintenance of the relation is always dependent on contributions from both parties. True, from the perspective of virtue theory, the carer gets the lion's share of moral credit. But from the care perspective, a huge thank-you goes to the responsive children, the students glowing with new learning, the feeble elderly who can do little more than smile a thanks for efforts at care. We know just how great these contributions are when they are withdrawn.

Insisting on the relational sense of caring (while not discarding the virtue sense) does make the philosophical case more complex. But it brings us face to face with real moral life. How good I can be depends at least in part on how you treat me. My goodness is not entirely my property, and the control I exercise as a carer is always a shared control.

Curriculum and Moral Education

In this part of the book, theoretical issues are explored a bit further, but each chapter addresses practical classroom applications as well. Chapter 9 picks up again on John Dewey's first meaning of moral education; that is, it asks what constitutes a moral education—one that is morally justifiable. The claim here is that schooling is a multipurpose enterprise, that it cannot restrict itself to the promotion of academic competence. It must address what is often called the whole child, but even more than that, it must prepare that child for the full range of activities in which all adults engage. It has to set the conditions under which it is both possible and attractive to be good.

In the chapters that follow, I am concerned with both the purposes (or aims) of moral education and its content. Chapter 10 looks at the role of schooling in helping students to understand their own inclinations toward good and evil; it takes a specifically feminist perspective. It is related to my full-length treatment in *Women and Evil* (Noddings, 1989).

Chapter 11 emphasizes the role of conversation in moral education. The point here is that we must live with our children and engage them in regular conversation if we are to affect their moral development. It is not a matter of simply instructing them on moral virtues and monitoring their behavior. We have to talk to them, listen to them, teach them the special language of moral life, and encourage their reflection on the great existential questions. As we do this, we promote the process of reflection in both our children and ourselves.

Chapter 12 discusses how we might use stories to promote such discussion. In the use of stories, we see a strong resemblance between care theory's approach to moral education and that of character education. The similarity is clear. But so, I hope, are the differences. There is no suggestion that moral education should be separated from the regular school subjects, although it is no secret that I—like many others—would like to see a thorough reorganization of the school curriculum. However, so long as we are faced with the standard disciplines, we should find ways to include moral education as part of each subject. Moral education is thus acknowledged as part of every human activity, and the disciplines themselves are enriched by the stories we tell.

A Morally Defensible Mission for Schools in the 21st Century

THE SOCIAL CHANGES in the years since World War II have been enormous. We have seen changes in work patterns, in residential stability, in style of housing, in sexual mores, in dress, in manners, in language, in music, in entertainment, and—perhaps most important of all—in family arrangements. While schools have responded, albeit sluggishly, to technological changes with various additions to curriculum and narrowly prescribed methods of instruction, they have largely ignored massive social changes. When they *have* responded, they have done so in piecemeal fashion, addressing isolated bits of the problem. Thus, recognizing that some children come to school hungry, schools provide meals for poor children. Alarmed by the increase in teenage pregnancies and sexually transmitted diseases, schools provide sex education. Many more examples could be offered, but none of the reforms, individually or collectively, adequately meets the educational needs of today's students.

What do we want for our children? What do they need from education, and what does our society need? The popular response today is that students need more academic training, that the country needs more people with greater mathematical and scientific competence, that a more adequate academic preparation will save people from poverty, crime, and other evils of current society. Most of these claims are either false or, at best, only partly true. For example, we do not need more physicists and mathematicians; many people already highly trained in these fields are unable to find work. Most adults do not use algebra in their work, and forcing all students to study it is a simplistic response to the real issues of equity and mathematical literacy. Just as clearly, more education will not save people from poverty unless a sufficient number of unfortunate people either reject that education or are squeezed out of it. Not everyone can obtain one of the jobs that our society now rewards adequately. There are limited numbers of such jobs, and even if everyone were well educated, some people would have to do the essential work that is underpaid at present. Thus education cannot be the route out of poverty for everyone. Poverty is a *social* problem, not merely an educational one. No person who does honest, useful work—regardless of his or her educational attainments—should live in poverty. A society that allows this to happen is not an educational failure; it is a moral failure.

Our society does not need to make its children first in the world in mathematics and science. It needs to care for its children—to reduce violence, to respect honest work of every kind, to reward excellence at every level, to ensure a place for every child and emerging adult in the economic and social world, to produce people who can care competently for their own families and contribute effectively to their communities. In direct opposition to the current emphasis on academic standards, a national curriculum, and national assessment, I have argued that our main educational aim should be to encourage the growth of competent, caring, loving, and lovable people (Noddings, 1992).

At the present time, it is obvious that our main educational purpose is not the moral one of producing caring people but a relentless—and, as it turns out, hapless—drive for academic adequacy. I am certainly not going to argue for academic *in*adequacy, but I will try to persuade readers that a reordering of priorities is essential. All children must learn to care for other human beings, and all must find an ultimate concern in some center of care: care for self, for intimate others, for associates and acquaintances, for distant others, for animals, for plants and the physical environment, for objects and instruments, and for ideas. Within each of these centers, we can find many themes on which to build courses, topical seminars, projects, reading lists, and dialogue.

Today the curriculum is organized almost entirely around the last center, ideas, but it is so poorly put together that important ideas are often swamped by facts and skills. Even those students who might find a genuine center of care in some arena of ideas—say mathematics or literature—are sorely disappointed. In trying to teach everyone what we once taught only a few, we have wound up teaching everyone inadequately. Further, we have not bothered to ask whether the traditional education so highly treasured was ever the best education for anyone.

I have argued that liberal education (defined as a set of traditional disciplines) is an outmoded and dangerous model of education for today's young. The popular slogan today is, All children can learn. To insist, however, that all children should get the same dose of academic English, social studies, science, and mathematics invites an important question not addressed by the sloganeers: *Why* should children learn what we insist they "can" learn? Is this the material people really need to live intelligently, morally, and happily? Or are arguments for traditional liberal education badly mistaken? Worse, are they perhaps mere political maneuverings?

My argument against liberal education is not a complaint against literature, history, physical science, mathematics, or any other subject. It is an argument, first, against an ideology of control that forces all students to study a particular, narrowly prescribed curriculum devoid of content they might truly care about. Second, it is an argument in favor of greater respect for a wonderful range of human capacities now largely ignored in schools. Third, it is an argument against the persistent undervaluing of skills, attitudes, and capacities traditionally associated with women. This last is an argument that has been eloquently made by Jane Roland Martin (1995).

What do we want for our children? Most of us hope that our children will find someone to love, find useful work they enjoy or at least do not hate, establish a family, and maintain bonds with friends and relatives. These hopes are part of our interest in shaping an acceptable child. What kind of mates, parents, friends, and neighbors will our children be?

I would hope that all of our children—both girls and boys—would be prepared to do the work of attentive love. This work must be done in every family situation, whether the family is conventionally or unconventionally constituted. Both men and women, if they choose to be parents, should participate in the joys and responsibilities of direct parenting, of acting as psychological parent. Too often, women have complained about bearing this responsibility almost entirely. When men volunteer to help with childcare or help with housework, the very language suggests that the tasks are women's responsibilities. Men "help" in tasks they do not perceive as their own. That has to change.

In education today, there is great concern about women's participation in mathematics and science. Some researchers even refer to something called the "problem of women and mathematics." Women's lack of success or low rate of participation in fields long dominated by men is seen as a problem to be treated by educational means. But researchers do not seem to see a problem in men's low rate of participation in nursing, elementary school teaching, or full-time parenting. Our society values activities traditionally associated with men above those traditionally associated with women.

The new education I envision puts a very high value on the traditional occupations of women. Care for children, the aged, and the ill must be shared by all capable adults, not just women, and everyone should understand that these activities bring special rewards as well as burdens. Work with children can be especially rewarding and provides an opportunity to enjoy childhood vicariously. For example, I have often wondered why high school students are not more often invited to revisit the literature of child-hood in their high school English classes. A careful study of fairy tales, augmented by essays on their psychology, might be more exciting and more generally useful than, for example, the study of *Hamlet*. When we consider the natural interest we have in ourselves—past, present, and future—it is clear that literature that allows us to look forward and backward is won-derful. Further, the study of fairy tales would provide opportunities for lessons in geography, history, art, and music.

Our children should learn something about life cycles and stages. When I was in high school, my Latin class read Cicero's essay "On Old Age." With all his talk of wisdom—of milk, honey, wine, and cheese, of meditating in the afternoon breeze—I was convinced that old age had its own romance. Looking at the present condition of many elderly people, I see more than enough horror to balance whatever romance there may be. But studies of early childhood, adulthood, and old age (with or without Latin) seem central to education for real life. Further, active association with people of all ages should be encouraged. Again, one can see connections with standard subjects—statistical studies in math; the history and sociol-ogy of welfare, medical care, and family life; geographical and cultural differences. We see, also, that the need for such studies has increased as a result of the social changes discussed earlier. Home life does not provide the experience in these areas that it once did.

Relations with intimate others are the beginning and one of the sig-nificant ends of moral life. If we regard our relations with intimate oth-ers as central in moral life, then we must provide all our children with practice in caring. Children can work together formally and informally on a host of school projects and, as they get older, they can help younger children, contribute to the care of building and grounds, and eventually—under careful supervision—do volunteer work in the community. Look-ing at Howard Gardner's (1983) multiple intelligences, we see that chil-dren can contribute useful service in a wide variety of ways; some have artistic talents, some interpersonal gifts, some athletic or kinesthetic abili-ties, some spiritual gifts.

A moral policy, a defensible mission, for education recognizes a mul-tiplicity of human capacities and interests. Instead of preparing every-one for college in the name of democracy and equality, schools should instill in students a respect for all forms of honest work done well (J. Gardner, 1961). Preparation for the world of work, for parenting, and for civic responsibility is essential for all students. All of us must work, but few of us do the sort of work that requires preparation in algebra and geometry. Almost all of us enter into intimate relationships, but schools largely ignore the centrality of such interests in our lives. And although most of us become parents, evidence suggests that we are not very good at parenting—and again the schools largely ignore this huge human task.

When I suggest that a morally defensible mission for education necessarily focuses on matters of human caring, people sometimes agree but fear the loss of an intellectual mission for the schools. There are at least two powerful responses to this fear. First, anyone who supposes that the current drive for uniformity in standards, curriculum, and assessment represents an intellectual agenda needs to reflect on the matter. Indeed, many thoughtful educators insist that such moves are truly anti-intellectual, discouraging critical thinking, creativity, and novelty. Second, and more important from the perspective adopted here, a curriculum centered on themes of care can be as richly intellectual as we and our students want to make it. Those of us advocating genuine reform—indeed, transformation—will surely be accused of anti-intellectualism, just as John Dewey was in the middle of the 20th century. But the accusation is false, and we should have the courage to face it down.

Examples of themes that are especially important to young people include love and friendship. Both can be studied in intellectual depth, but the crucial emphasis should be on the relevance of the subjects to self-understanding and growth. Friends are especially important to teenagers, and they need guidance in making and maintaining friendships.

Aristotle wrote eloquently on friendship, and he assessed it as central in moral life. In the *Nicomachean Ethics*, Aristotle wrote that the main criterion of friendship is that a friend wishes a friend well for his or her own sake. When we befriend others, we want good things for them not because those things may enhance our welfare but because they are good for our friends. Aristotle organized friendships into various categories: those motivated by common business or political purposes, those maintained by common recreational interests, and those created by mutual admiration of the other's virtue. The last was, for Aristotle, the highest form of friendship and, of course, the one most likely to endure.

How do friendships occur? What draws people together? Here students should have opportunities to see how far Aristotle's description will carry them. They should hear about Damon and Pythias, of course. But they should also examine some incongruous friendships. Huck and Jim in Mark Twain's *Adventures of Huckleberry Finn*; Miss Celie and Shug in Alice Walker's *The Color Purple*; Lenny and George in John Steinbeck's *Of Mice and Men*; Jane and Maudie in Doris Lessing's *Diaries of Jane Somers*. What does each of these characters give to the friendship? Can friendship be part of a personal quest for fulfillment? When does a personal objective go too far and negate Aristotle's basic criterion?

Another issue to be considered is, When should moral principles outweigh the demands of friendship? The question is often cast this way, even though many of us find the wording misleading. What the questioner wants us to consider is whether we should protect friends who have done something morally wrong. A few years ago, there was a terrifying example of this problem when a teenage boy killed a girl and bragged about it to his friends. His friends, in what they interpreted as an act of loyalty, did not even report the murder.

From the perspective of caring, there is no inherent conflict between moral requirements and friendship, because, as Aristotle teaches us, we have a primary obligation to promote our friends' moral growth. But lots of concrete conflicts can arise when we have to consider exactly what to do. Instead of juggling principles, as we might when we say, "Friendship is more important than a little theft," or "Murder is more important than friendship," we begin by asking ourselves whether the acts our friends have committed are caring acts. If they are not, and the consequences are serious, something has to be done. In the case of something as horrible as murder, the act must be reported. But true friends would also go beyond initial judgment and action to ask how they can follow through with appropriate help for the murderer. When we adopt caring as an ethical approach, our moral work has just begun where other approaches end. Caring requires staying-with, or what Ruddick (1989) has called "holding." We do not let our friends fall if we can help it, and if they do, we hold on and pull them back up.

Gender differences in friendship patterns should also be discussed. It may be harder for males to reject relationships in which they are pushed to do socially unacceptable acts, because those acts are often used as tests of manhood. Females, by contrast, find it more difficult to separate themselves from abusive relationships. In both cases, young people have to learn not only to take appropriate responsibility for the moral growth of others but also to insist that others accept responsibility for their own behavior. It is often a fine line, and—since there are no formulas to assist us—we remain vulnerable in all our moral relations.

A transformation of the sort envisioned here requires organizational and structural changes to support the changes in curriculum and instruction. It requires a move away from the ideology of control, from the mistaken notion that ironhanded accountability will ensure the outcomes we identify as desirable. It just won't happen. We should have learned by now that both children and adults can accomplish wonderful things in an atmosphere of love and trust and that they will (if they are healthy) resist—sometimes to their own detriment—in environments of coercion.

Because I would like to present for discussion my basic recommendations for both structural and curricular changes, I will risk setting them forth here in a skeletal form. Of course, I cannot describe and defend the recommendations adequately in so brief a space, but here is a summary.

The traditional organization of schooling is intellectually and morally inadequate for contemporary society. We live in an age troubled by social problems that force us to reconsider what we do in schools. Too many of us think that we can improve education by merely designing a better curriculum, finding and implementing a better form of instruction, or instituting a better form of classroom management. These things won't work.

We need to give up the notion of a single ideal of the educated person and replace it with a multiplicity of models designed to accommodate the multiple capacities and interests of students. We need to recognize multiple identities. For example, an 11th-grader may be a Black, a woman, a teenager, a Smith, an American, a New Yorker, a Methodist, a person who loves math, and so on. As she exercises these identities, she may use different languages, adopt different postures, and relate differently to those around her. But whoever she is at a given moment, whatever she is engaged in, she needs—as we all do—to be cared for. Her need for care may require formal respect, informal interaction, expert advice, just a flicker of recognition, or sustained affection. To give the care she needs requires a set of capacities in each of us to which schools give too little attention.

I have argued that education should be organized around themes of care rather than the traditional disciplines. All students should be engaged in a general education that guides them in caring for self, intimate others, global others, plants, animals, the environment, objects and instruments, and ideas. Moral life so defined should be frankly embraced as the main goal of education. Such an aim does not work against intellectual development or academic achievement. Rather, it supplies a firm foundation for both.

How can we begin? Here is what I think we must do:

1. *Be clear and unapologetic about our goal.* The main aim of education should be to produce competent, caring, loving, and lovable people.

2. *Take care of affiliative needs.* We must keep students and teachers together (by mutual consent) for several years, and we must keep students together when possible. We should also strive to keep students in the same building for considerable periods of time and help students to think of the

school as their own. Finally, we must legitimize time spent on building relations of care and trust.

3. *Relax the impulse to control.* We need to give teachers and students more responsibility to exercise judgment. At the same time, we must get rid of competitive grading and reduce the amount of testing that we do. Those well-designed tests that remain should be used to assess whether people can competently handle the tasks they want to undertake. We also need to encourage teachers to explore material with students. We don't have to know everything to teach well.

In short, we need to define expertise more broadly and instrumentally. For example, a biology teacher should be able to teach whatever mathematics is involved in biology, and a social studies teacher should be able to teach whatever mathematics is required in that subject. We must encourage self-evaluation and teach students how to do it competently, and we must also involve students in governing their own classrooms and schools. Making such changes means that we accept the challenge to care by teaching well the things that students want to learn.

4. *Get rid of program hierarchies.* This will take time, but we must begin now to provide excellent programs for *all* our children. Programs for the noncollege-bound should be just as rich, desirable, and rigorous as those for the college-bound.

We must abandon uniform requirements for college entrance. What a student wants to do or to study should guide what is required by way of preparation. Here we should not worry greatly about students "changing their minds." Right now we are so afraid that if students prepare for something particular, they may change their minds and all that preparation will be wasted. Thus we busily prepare them uniformly for nothing. We forget that when people have a goal in mind, they learn well, and that even if they change their minds, they may well have acquired the skills and habits of mind they will need for further learning. The one essential point is that we give all students what all students need—genuine opportunities to explore the questions central to human life.

5. *Give at least part of every day to themes of care.* We should discuss existential questions—including spiritual matters—freely. Moreover, we need to help students learn to treat one another ethically by giving them practice in caring. We must help students understand how groups and individuals create rivals and enemies and help them learn how to "be on both sides." We should encourage a way of caring for animals, plants, and the environment that is consistent with caring for humans, and we should also encourage caring for the human-made world. Students need to feel at home in technical, natural, and cultural worlds, and educators must cultivate wonder and appreciation for the human-made world.

6. *Teach students that caring in every domain implies competence.* When we care, we accept the responsibility to work continuously on our competence so that the recipient of our care—person, animal, object, or idea—is enhanced. There is nothing mushy about caring. It is the strong, resilient backbone of human life.

Educating Moral People

FROM A FEMINIST PERSPECTIVE, it does not seem credible that the aim of education in current cultures is to produce good people, even though there is much talk about doing exactly that. Indeed, I will argue that a female view reveals that our educational practices have been designed to produce people who, in at least one respect, are *not* good—who are inclined to violence and are unreflective about the ethical codes that support their violent inclinations. I will begin by examining differences between stereotypical masculine and feminine views on good and evil, and then argue that analysis and elaboration of an authentic female perspective can contribute greatly to our understanding of moral life. Finally, I will sketch a program for the inclusion of both female and male moral perspectives in the school curriculum, first with respect to developing the good, and then with attention to the control of evil.

CONFLICT OVER GOOD AND EVIL

The feminist perspective that I will use has a long history. It has sometimes been called "social" or "maternal" feminism (Black, 1983) and has in the past even been identified with a "redemptive" function of motherhood (see Bernard, 1975, ch. 18). Its most significant and lasting feature has been an insistence that the logic of women's experience implies a strong stand against violence (Black, 1983). Contemporary feminists who have much in common with earlier maternal feminists (which is not to say there are no differences) may be found among both radical feminists (Daly, 1984) and psychoanalytic feminists (Dinnerstein, 1976; Chodorow, 1978). A few of them present arguments that strongly resemble those of their maternal feminist forebears but show considerably more analytic sophistication (Ruddick, 1980, 1984, 1989). This perspective acknowledges that there are still substantial differences between men and women, including differences in their views on moral life.

It does not, however, attribute all the differences to biology and nature but traces many of them to centuries of different experience.

In this it differs from the position of the Jungians, who attribute differences in male and female assessments of good and evil to differences in essential nature. Because I want to adapt several important insights from Jung and his followers, it is necessary to say at the outset that I reject the Jungian notion of essential, predetermined, and opposite feminine and masculine natures. Some Jungians, for example, go so far as to say that men and women are mirror opposites in their spiritual evaluations. Esther Harding (1976) declares, "That which to man is spiritual, good, and to be sought after, is to woman demonic, powerful, and destructive, and vice versa" (p. 36). This view has done great mischief by locking women and men into values that should be reevaluated as candidates for *human* views of good and evil.

Both women and men have been greatly influenced by stereotypical images of the feminine and the masculine. Our society has set its expectations along stereotypical lines. From this perspective, it has been acceptable for women to deplore war and violence and for men to define themselves in various forms of combat. The male view has, however, been dominant, and women have been called upon to support the warrior code of honor, even though the code represents, for them, a call to evil. When they do not help men to "behave honorably," women are blamed, and often blame themselves, for what is perceived as moral failure. Harding writes, "The typical story is that he must join his regiment. When he goes to say goodbye to her she coaxes him to remain or is so alluring he forgets his obligation, and the army entrains without him" (1976, p. 81).

But instead of evaluating women's tendency to put relation before all else as a possible good to be considered by both women and men, as an intuition to be rationally elaborated into a coherent position, Harding claims, "All true women blame the woman who acts in this way, rather than the man. They know that such an action takes unfair advantage of man's vulnerability" (1976, p. 81).

This judgment reveals a Jungian belief in the great power of the feminine, but it is here construed as the power of the temptress—the "devil's gateway." Perhaps the most damaging effect of the warrior code on women has been the universal devaluation of virtues thought to be peculiarly feminine. The "law of kindness," for example, is assessed as virtuous so long as it is confined to home and immediate community but is considered evil if it opposes the warrior code (consider the expression "giving aid and comfort to the enemy").

Because they conflict with the warrior code, women's virtues (compassion, responsiveness, tenderness, and the like) have been assessed as weaknesses in public life. Further, weakness itself has long been associated with the "eternal feminine." Paul Ricoeur (1969) speaks of an "eternal feminine which is more than sex and which might be called the *mediation of the weakness*, the frailty of man" (p. 254). While insisting that this eternal feminine as frailty does not point only at women but at all humankind, he completes his argument with the well-known quotation from *Hamlet*: "Frailty, thy name is woman." Hence "weakness" and "woman" are synonymous. In many cultures, our own included, it has been, and still is, a terrible insult to call a man "womanish" or to say that he thinks like a woman.

Hatred of feminine attributes has sometimes even induced hatred of religious institutions, which represent a component of public life that seems to edify these virtues. Nietzsche, for example, lumped both Christianity and women's thinking together into something he called a "slave mentality." Christian churchmen, he said,

> Smash the strong, contaminate great hopes, cast suspicion on joy in beauty, break down everything autocratic, manly, conquering, tyrannical, all the instincts proper to the highest and most successful of the type "man," into uncertainty, remorse of conscience, self-destruction, indeed reverse the whole love of the earthly and dominion over the earth into hatred of the earth and the earthly. (1973, p. 70)

As we shall see shortly, there is much that feminists might agree with in Nietzsche's critique of the church's condemnation of all that is earthly. But Nietzsche has profoundly misinterpreted the church and its real purpose and activities. While it has *preached* what Nietzsche regards as a slave mentality, it has for the most part lived in "autocratic, manly, conquering, tyrannical" ways. With a few significant exceptions, it has remained firmly a part of the warrior mode, and this, from the perspective taken here, is far more evil than a slave mentality.

Outstanding male objectors to the warrior model should be mentioned; these would certainly include Jesus and Gandhi. Each of these men preached nonviolence, loving kindness, and restraint in the pursuit of justice, but each revealed peculiar weaknesses in his private life. Gandhi, for example, seems to have exercised a good bit of psychological violence in his personal life. In his study of Gandhi, Erik Erikson says that he sensed "the presence of a kind of untruth in the very protestation of truth; of something unclean when all the words spelled out an unreal purity; and, above all, of displaced violence where nonviolence was the professed issue" (1969, pp. 230–231). Jesus, while counseling his followers against violence, promised that God would mete out justice in destruction of the wicked. Even his commandment to love one another is ambivalent; in its content, it clearly opposes the warrior code, but in its form—as commandment—it strongly reflects the code. The mother-god might simply say, "I ask you to be gentle with my other children for I love them dearly, too." Recognition of the failure of intimacy that has often accompanied male expressions of universal love and abstract justice is necessary in building an authentic female ethic. In their rejection of physical violence, these men did not completely reject the warrior model; rather, they translated it into a psychological model that still retains power as its goal.

We might, indeed, argue that religious descriptions of evil (by male authorities) have served to mask real evils and even to endorse them. Certainly, they have made women scapegoats for the origin of evil, and the set of myths that accomplished this has demeaned both women and the values they embrace. Mary Daly says of the Adamic myth:

> [T]he myth takes on cosmic proportions since the male's viewpoint is metamorphosed into God's viewpoint. It amounts to a cosmic false naming. It misnames the mystery of evil, casting it into the distorted mold of the myth of feminine evil. In this way images and conceptualizations about evil are thrown out of focus and its deepest dimensions are not really confronted. (1974, p. 47)

The harm that has been done by the misnaming of evil is incalculable. First, of course, it has inflicted harm on both men and women, but especially on women, by evaluating the earth, body, woman, and nature as lower than heaven, mind, man, and spirit. The devaluation of earth and material interests is one of Nietzsche's great complaints against Christianity, and it is a complaint many feminists share.

Second, it has legitimated the infliction of suffering. Since a God thought to be all-powerful and all-good allows suffering in the world (and even supposedly inflicts it to teach us valuable lessons), human beings have found reasons to justify their own infliction of pain and suffering on one another. For all his opposition to the Christian slave mentality of suffering and sacrifice, Nietzsche—hewing to the warrior model—does not find the infliction or undergoing of suffering objectionable. Rather, he elevates suffering to the status of a criterion for greatness.

Third, because the Augustinian tradition has decreed that the perfection of the universe requires "misery for sinners" (Augustine, 1964), people have projected evil (or sin) onto those whom they would hurt or destroy. Nowhere is this more obvious than in preparation for war, which seems to require almost a frenzy of hatred toward people branded as subhuman, evil, or even monstrous. The need to project evil onto others in order to exteriorize it and thus to destroy it without blaming the self has been turned on women and other "inferiors" as well as on enemies (Daly, 1974, p. 76). This point seems to have been especially well understood by Jung and some of his followers (Neumann, 1955; von Franz, 1983), and I will return to it in the last section.

Fourth, and finally for present purposes, the notion that evil cannot be in God or, by implication, in oneself except insofar as one separates himself or herself from God, leads to a dangerous neglect of what Jungians call our "shadow." If we pretend, for example, that we are all-loving, suppressing our inclinations to hate, we may experience an enantiodromia—a dramatic flow of energy from the pole of love to the pole of hate (Jung, [reprint] 1969). An outburst of violence might be the eventual result. Jung, therefore, suggests that a "morality of evil" (ibid., pp. 434, 457) is needed if we are to learn how to control the shadow side. In contrast to Jung's view, which is often considered feminine, Nietzsche—the ultimate masculinist— recommended the incorporation of our devils, or shadow, in order to become more powerful (see Barrett, 1962, pp. 177–205).

In summary, the traditional (masculine) view of evil took the natural association of evil with pain, terror, separation, death, and destruction and transformed it into "ethical terror" (Ricoeur, 1969)—fear of transgressing against the patriarch (God, father, church, or state). Thus it misnamed, or covered up, the true nature of evil (Noddings, 1989). In its collaboration with the warrior model, this traditional view may even be accused of participating in evil. Thus there is an analytical task for feminists not only in raising the value of virtues once thought to be feminine but also in redefining and describing evil. Rosemary Radford Ruether says, "Feminism represents a fundamental shift in the valuations of good and evil. It makes a fundamental judgment upon aspects of past descriptions of the nature and etiology of evil as themselves ratifications of evil" (1983, p. 160).

THE NEED FOR A FEMALE PERSPECTIVE

Different outlooks on good and evil lead, logically, to different prescriptions for goodness and for moral education. One would expect considerable overlap in male and female prescriptions as a result of a common culture, but because the female view has not been well articulated in the past, mere overlap is often construed as consensus. In part, the lack of articulation is a direct result of the male conception of woman's goodness: silence and service. It is imperative, then, to return to situations that have been analyzed through traditional perspectives and examine them from the viewpoint of women's experience. This involves a reevaluation of both masculine and feminine traits.

In contrast to Harding's judgment that a woman who distracts her lover from duty and honor is "a public menace" (1976, p. 82), we might want to investigate carefully the moral status of such acts and their underlying premises. This is not a simple matter of dismissing a man's obligation to his fellows on the ground that war is evil in itself; nor is it a matter of declaring women morally justified a priori when they distract men from battle. The proposed program must recognize that there are men who find war glorious, others who defect out of pure self-interest, and still others who go reluctantly but dutifully into battle. It must recognize, also, that there are women who play seductress for their own narrow ends. But, when mean motives are stripped away, there are genuine ethical insights to be found. Uncovering them requires a detailed phenomenological analysis, which must be guided by such questions as the following: What does the woman dread (beyond the loss of her man, his injury, her loneliness)? What tempts the man to defect (beyond the present sexual temptation)? What presses the woman to let him go? What drives him to leave? An exploration of these questions might reveal a deeply shared set of basic intuitions—that to be together sharing a life and building a family and community is better than to be alone or with valued others who are pledged to destruction; that a man who kills may never be quite like one who has not killed; that killing one who does not wish to die is somehow deeply wrong no matter who does it or in what cause; that human beings often fear the condemnation of their peers even more than death and loss; that separation induces the risk of lost love; that one's courage may fail and that one is not sure what courage is; that neglect of relation is itself a great evil (something we all once knew in our early fears of abandonment); that all people in a situation like ours, even those we are about to engage in combat, feel these things. All of these intuitions can be incorporated into a powerful ethical position that supports woman's way of being in the world as rational rather than weak or self-serving.

It is important to understand that it is not the purpose of such an analysis to claim or to demonstrate the moral superiority of women. No such claim is necessary. The aim is to pay attention to a perspective on ethical life that is available to us through women's experience and that may help all of us lead better lives. Daniel Maguire puts the matter well when he says, "Because the experience of women has given them certain advantages in their moral perceptivity, their exclusion from most centers of power in most civilizations has impoverished the species" (1982, pp. 59–60). I must add, however, that it is not just the exclusion of women that impoverishes the species; it is also the deprivation of experience in men. Because women's work, attitudes, and ways of thinking have been despised, men have avoided the sort of experience common to women. Therefore, the suggested analysis must probe women's experience for intuitions that may, with some modification, be shared by both men and women.

As the basic intuitions are uncovered, the value ascribed to them can be traced to tribal experience, as the Jungians have held. In contrast to the Jungians, however, we need not trace these differences beyond experience to essential differences in nature. This leaves open the possibility of both reconciliation and transcendence, while recognizing the difficulty of the enterprise. Men and women may be reconciled in appreciation of their differing experience and commitments; but they may also transcend the differences by a heroic effort to uncover what lies shared beneath the surface conflicts. What is it that man values in war? If it is power (macho-masculinity, tyranny), then we must reject it and call it evil, because it induces pain, separation, and helplessness. If it is faithfulness, adventure, challenge, and courage, then men and women may ask, How else can these aims and virtues be encouraged and indulged?

This begins to sound like a search for what William James called "the moral equivalent of war: something heroic that will speak to men as universally as war does, and yet will be as compatible with their spiritual selves as war has proved itself to be incompatible" (1902/1929, p. 359). But James's statement suggests that he sought the motivational, not the moral, equivalent of war. His choice of words is, however, entirely consonant with the warrior model and underscores my claim that the experience of men and women has been fundamentally different. Although he recognizes the incompatibility of war with a spiritual self, he still says, "Yet the fact remains that war is a school of strenuous life and heroism; and, being in the line of aboriginal instinct, is the only school that as yet is universally available" (p. 359).

Women, looking at their own universe, might point to motherhood (also in line with aboriginal experience) as a school universally accessible and one that teaches very different lessons—lessons of tenderness, empowerment, and constancy (Gilligan, 1982; Noddings, 1984; Ruddick, 1980). But James does not see this alternative. Indeed, he pursues the paradox of war's horror and glory by commenting, "But when we gravely ask ourselves whether this wholesale organization of irrationality and crime be our only bulwark against effeminacy, we stand aghast at the thought, and think more kindly of ascetic religion" (p. 359). Having the softer qualities of a woman is something against which men need a bulwark; it is not considered an alternative mode that has its own contribution to make to universal heroism. Indeed, a turn to ascetic religion as suggested by James reveals yet another familiar litany of "goods" that are accompanied by outcomes often regarded as evil by women: isolation and neglect of interpersonal relations, distrust and even abuse of the body and its desires, passionate attachment to abstraction and ritual instead of concrete others, a rejection of personal love in favor of universal love. James fears some of these, too, and is not entirely approving in his analysis of asceticism, but he fears "effeminacy" even more.

The long-standing fear of being like a woman or being captured by a woman has led men—even intelligent, open-minded men like James—to suppose that male experience must somehow be defined in opposition to female experience. James, who declared himself a pacifist and clearly deplored the horrors of war, was unable to let go of the male notions of "hardihood," "manliness," "striving," and the like. He found it necessary to cast about for experiential domains and activities that would provide a suitable arena for masculine prowess. I am not suggesting that virtues and traits honored by men be simply discarded; rather, I am suggesting that they be analyzed anew from the perspective of women so that both women and men can be relieved of the burden of stereotypical expectations and of the violence and oppression that accompany them.

To articulate a feminine morality requires analysis of several kinds: first, the analysis of relational phenomena, such as caring (Noddings, 1984) and response (Gilligan, 1982); second, the analysis of situations that have been used in the past to explicate male consciousness; third, the analysis of situations, tasks, and relations that are central to female experience; and fourth, the analysis of connections among the first three. What are the connections, if any, among the cultural and biological experience of women and (1) relational phenomena, such as caring, response, and tenderness, and (2) the traits, behaviors, and linguistic expressions that appear in situations already analyzed from the male perspective?

Such analysis may well press a dialectic between male and female views of morality, and the outcome of a vigorous dialectic should be a fuller and clearer vision of what it means to be a good person. It may also provide us with material to build Jung's much-needed "morality of evil." It is clear that at the present time most men would not regard themselves as fully human persons if they adopted a "feminine" moral attitude and, just as clearly, most women would not regard themselves as good if they employed the male mode exclusively.

LEARNING THE MANLY AND WOMANLY ARTS

Because the universal has been described by males, and culture has been created or at least interpreted by men, schools are pervaded by male language and structures. Although the manly arts of the warrior are no longer extensively and explicitly taught, they are embedded in literature and political history, in sports, in a controlling view of science, in academic contests, in the hierarchical structure of school districts, and in competition for grades. It is not just the presence of football teams and ROTC on campuses that mark male dominance; rather, the standard curriculum itself may be characterized as a masculine project (Grumet, 1988).

I am not going to argue that it is wrong for boys (or girls) to learn the manly arts, but I do think it is wrong for them to be uncritically initiated into the warrior mode. Stories like *The Iliad* and *The Odyssey* have been used for centuries to introduce young men to the virtues of the warrior model and young women to the model of the faithful wife. These stories need not be abandoned, but they should be examined critically: their characters and plots should not be allowed to stand as uncriticized exemplars of virtue. Further, young people should be encouraged to consider whether the tragic events in these stories are evil tricks of fate or whether they result from the warrior model itself—something evil embedded in it that ensures a continuous cycle of tragedy. Such critical examination is vitally important at the present time, because the differential effects of these stories on boys and girls may be fading. More and more, girls want access to the public world, and they may, quite understandably, emulate virtues that are presented to them as *human* virtues, even if those virtues are incompatible with the spiritual attitudes they have inherited from the maternal model.

Many people today, even many feminists, espouse an equity model. They assume that the cure for women's oppression is free and equitable access to the public world. They forget, however, that the public world has been defined and built by men. The standards and practices have been established by males, and thus it is a male model women must adopt in availing themselves of free access. It is as though men were to say, Here, now, we know that we have been unfair; we will now share our power and work with you; all you have to do is show that you're up to it. It is an unintentionally arrogant model that presupposes women want to be like men and just need the chance to grow in that direction. While I would not argue against equity, I would advise against a blind striving for equity without transformation; that is, I would argue against accepting equity in a model that promotes—and even glorifies—domination and oppression. The fundamental assumption here is that to be human is to be male.

An alternative is to analyze the structures and practices of our society from the perspective of women's experience and to begin the complex process of constructing a genuinely universal interpretation of culture. This is an extraordinarily difficult task, and only a few thinkers are working seriously at it. Jane Roland Martin (1984, 1985), for example, has suggested that we need to rethink our conception of the educated person, and our new ideal should be guided by a consideration of both "productive" and "reproductive" functions. She introduces these terms in a discussion of Plato's *Republic*:

> A fascinating feature of the experiment in thought in which Socrates and his friends construct the Just State is that the reproductive processes of society are all but ignored. Socrates knows that in addition to cobblers, shipbuilders, and cowherds a state needs to have children born and reared, houses cared for, the sick and elderly tended, and everyone fed. Yet he mentions . . . occupations traditionally performed by females—only in passing. (1985, p. 14)

I agree wholeheartedly with Martin's call for a new conception of the educated person, but I find her use of "productive" and "reproductive" problematic. The terms are usually found in Marxist contexts and thus point to the economic status of the two sets of tasks; this emphasis does not serve Martin's purposes well. We cannot be sure, for example, whether childrearing in Martin's conceptual scheme moves from the reproductive to the productive when it becomes paid work, nor does that move matter to Martin in the way it would to a Marxist. We might infer from the body of Martin's work that it is not so much the tasks themselves that demarcate the productive and the reproductive, but rather a set of attitudes brought to the work; she herself identifies "caring, compassion, and connection" (1985, p. 197). But if this is so, it underscores the need for a phenomenology of female experience, because these attitudes—this way of being in the world—have grown out of a relation to the tasks known as women's work. As Martin points out, simply to say, for example, that we will now attend to the three Cs in school without studying and somehow including the activities that give rise to them is to fall into a peculiarly traditional abstractionism.

Martin recognizes that we cannot solve the curricular problem by adding courses such as Compassion 101, and she is also wary of "replicating within the curriculum the split between the productive and reproductive processes of society" (1985, p. 197). She would, therefore, oppose relegating the three Cs to courses like home economics (but see Thompson, 1992, for rich possibilities in home economics). In this Martin is clearly right, but it may not be enough to attempt what she suggests as an alternative, namely, "incorporating Sophie's and Sarah's [female] virtues into our science, math, history, literature, and auto mechanics courses, even as we emphasize theoretical knowledge and the development of reason in the teaching of nutrition or family living" (1985, p. 198). The obstacles to dramatic change are so great, however, that I have made recommendations along the same lines.

The difficulty with this program is that it leaves the standard model very nearly intact; subject matter drawn from the traditional disciplines still reigns supreme. Martin recognizes this and has argued elsewhere for a dramatic change in subjects to be included in the curriculum. If we truly want a universally representative culture and education, we need to revise both the curriculum as a whole and internal elements of the curriculum. The new subjects of the curriculum must, further, stand on an equal footing with geometry and physics; they must not be accorded second-class status because they are developed from and reflect women's experience.

An example will illustrate the kind of change I see as necessary. Suppose we were to introduce a new subject called People: Their Growth, Customs, and Relationships. This would not be a one-semester course in anthropology, or social history, or psychology, or biology. Nor would it be interdisciplinary in the narrow sense of drawing directly and only upon these established disciplines. It would be an ongoing subject with its own integrity—one taught across the years as math and English now are, and it would have a practice component. At the high school level, freshmen might study the young child and work directly as helpers in preschools and kindergartens. The course of study would include a history of childhood, classic works of art pertaining to childhood, children's poetry and literature (what a wonderful opportunity to revisit loved stories from a "higher" standpoint), the biology and developmental psychology of childhood, and some cross-cultural sociology of childhood.

Sophomores might study old age and do their practice in nursing homes and adult communities. A study of political action might be introduced: Should the elderly have special rights? How will the social security system be maintained? What happens when a society focuses on its elderly instead of its young?

Juniors might study systems of religion and morality. This would provide an opportunity for young people to learn not only about other religions but, perhaps more important, about the political agendas that have accompanied the development of their own religious systems. Study would include the great Judeo-Christian myths, their pagan predecessors, and their roles in the oppression and liberation of women. Practice in this course might be chosen from a variety of possibilities ranging from work with a particular religious institution to work or study within a secular group interested in the influence and role of religion. In this area of curriculum reform, cries about the separation of church and state are sure to be heard (at least in the United States). The reaction should be neither defiance nor capitulation. Rather, both those who recognize the positive contributions of religion to our culture and those who are convinced that religious institutions have conspired to support the warrior model should gently and persistently press the case. A tremendous mystique has grown up around this mythical "separation," and it is time to engage in demystification.

In their last year of high school, students might study interpersonal relations, including sex, marriage, alternative life-styles, parenting, and friendship. Such courses already exist, of course, but not in the rich critical and practical patterns suggested here. All of these topics (and those of previous years as well) might be analyzed by examining the two great cultural models, warrior and mother.

This outline is, of course, a mere suggestion, and I am certainly not recommending that these topics—should they actually be selected—must be treated in this order. My main point is that subject matter can be defined and organized in a variety of ways. In particular, it can be organized around the topics that have been central to female experience. In a radical revision of education, the subjects themselves would be reconsidered and renamed in an attempt to achieve a vision of the humanities and sciences that would be more nearly universal. (I have been using the word "universal" in a descriptive, not prescriptive, sense; that is, I seek a cumulative description of moral life that includes voices long unheard in traditional attempts to build a universal prescriptive morality.)

I have argued that a new balance in education must draw as richly from female experience (in particular, the maternal model) as from male (the warrior model) and that this new balance requires a radical change in our conception of curriculum and subjects. In the meantime, the traditional subjects themselves must be reconsidered if children are to learn both the womanly and manly arts, and their learning must include both critical and appreciative analysis, as well as appropriate practical experience in living out these models.

Clearly, an emphasis on female experience implies significant changes in school structure and pedagogy as well as in curriculum, but I will concentrate here on curriculum. Two areas of the contemporary curriculum that might profit greatly from changes of content are English and social studies. I am not advocating the equity model, which, in its most simplistic form, would merely urge upon us an inclusion of women in standard public roles. In English, not only must women writers be sought out but women's themes must be treated. Very few of our students are asked to read Pearl Buck's *The Exile* (1936), for example, even though both this book (a biography of her mother) and *Fighting Angel* (1936), a biography of her father, were named in her Nobel award. *The Exile* is a magnificent story of the suffering and constancy of a Victorian mother forever in conflict between her devotion to particular, bodily human beings and the abstract God she was called upon to worship. It portrays the agony induced by a society and church that regard care and compassion for bodies as morally inferior to care and concern for souls. At bottom, the pair of books illustrates the clash between mother (the exile) and warrior (fighting angel) and demonstrates, too, that both virtues and vices, strengths and weaknesses are found in each model.

In social studies, a complete reconstruction is necessary. Students need to learn how to be good neighbors as well as informed voters. They need the history of families, housing arrangements, food production, childraising, volunteer work, social reform, and religion. They should learn about the heroism of women and men who have worked for reform in our treatment of the insane, the aged, immigrants, slaves, prisoners, workers, children, and animals. Furthermore, this material, so often buried in a few dull paragraphs, should be presented with drama and excitement, biography, and film.

The work to be done is enormous. Yet I agree with Jane Martin when she says that few tasks in education are as important or exciting (1985, p. 198). Martin also says that we should "not delude ourselves that education can be created anew" (1985, p. 198). This is certainly true of education seen as schooling. In our theoretical work, however, we *should* create education anew. The vision thus created can be used to guide the actual changes that we find feasible. Without such a vision, we grope blindly toward an unarticulated future. In achieving a fully human view of what it is to be a good person and in translating that view into an educational program, there is a need for a dialectic between male and female and also for one between the theoretical/ideal and the practical.

UNDERSTANDING AND CONTROLLING EVIL

Male and female conceptions of good and evil differ. In part, they differ because of the stereotypical expectations that have influenced all of us. A more interesting facet of the difference, however, appears when we see clearly how often and how dramatically men have defined themselves in opposition to all that is feminine. It is not just that women and men have been thought to be different but that maleness has been more often associated with the morally good and that evil has been defined in terms of disobedience to the patriarch. The analysis of women's experience with respect to evil may be even more important than the reevaluation of female virtues and traditional goodness. Again, it is vital to understand that this importance is not rooted in a claim for women's perfection. As Maguire points out, "Our sisters are not without sin" (1982, p. 62). Rather, one great contribution of women's perspective arises from the very fact that women have been subordinated and forced to think of their own shortcomings. In

Maguire's words, "[W]omen enjoy the wisdom that accrues to the alienated" (1982, p. 61). I am not sure "alienated" is the right word; "powerless" might be better. But his meaning is clear: The experience of subordination can produce wisdom as well as the attitude Nietzsche calls a slave mentality. This is not, of course, an argument for the continuation of women's subordination. Rather, it is an argument for reflection on this experience so that the wisdom accrued will not be lost as subordination is overcome.

Now that women are experiencing raised consciousness with respect to their long years of subordination, they are quite naturally interested in the political dimensions of programs and institutions, for example, the church, to which they have in the past given their uncritical devotion. As the religious heritage is examined, it becomes clear that dogma, doctrine, and custom have not grown solely out of spiritual concerns, nor have they served only spiritual purposes. The story of Eve, for example, has been used to justify men's subordination of women and, in particular, to justify their close control over women's sexuality (Phillips, 1984). Further, it now seems likely that parts of the Adam and Eve myth were designed to discredit and overthrow earlier female religions (Sanford, 1981; Stone, 1976). Looking at these stories with newly opened eyes, women are becoming keenly aware of the reasons and conditions under which evil has been defined as disobedience to the patriarch. This should be the right time, then, to undertake a phenomenology of evil from a female perspective.

What advantages might be found in using women's experience as a framework for the analysis of evil? First, women are in a peculiarly advantageous position to examine evil, because they have been treated as the other upon whom many evils have been projected (de Beauvoir, 1952; Harding, 1976). Second, because they have been relatively powerless to return the projection in the way that, say, two warring nations project evil on each other, they have learned to accept evil in themselves. Much of this is, of course, unwarranted, and I am not suggesting that the long association of women, materiality, and evil should be continued. It is neither the process of projection nor the projected content of evil that should be accepted, but rather the healthy process of striving to bring unconscious evil into consciousness rather than repressing and projecting it.

In this area, the work of Jung and his followers should prove very useful, for their analysis clearly reveals the danger in failing to recognize and understand the evil in ourselves. Jung ([reprint] 1969) even suggests that the Christian view of God as all-good needs to be revised to incorporate an evil side of the deity. In his recommendations for the conscious recognition of evil in both deity and human, Jung is not arguing for uncritical acceptance of evil or for a new power in performing evil deeds.

Rather, he is arguing that wholeness requires a controlled acceptance and understanding of the evil in ourselves and that this acceptance gives us some protection from actually committing evil.

Although there is wisdom in the Jungian teaching, there is also cause for feminist concern. When Jung discusses what is missing in the Christian view of God—what needs to be added to make a "whole" picture of God—he sometimes identifies the missing element as the evil side and sometimes identifies it as the feminine. Clearly, an uncritical reading of Jung could be used to sustain the traditional equation of women and evil. A more careful reading suggests that incorporation of the feminine may be a necessary prelude to the acceptance of evil in oneself and an end to projection of evil onto the other. When the other is an integral part of oneself, that which is there must be faced, controlled, improved, and treated with some respect. The experience of women in living as the other should, clearly, be a valuable resource in our study of wholeness and its relation to evil.

What does all this suggest for education? First, of course, it suggests the need to add feminine interpretations of the history of religion to our curriculum. It is critically important that young women and men learn what the Judeo-Christian tradition has done for them and to them. Any education that purports to be liberal is a fraud without this body of knowledge.

Second, it suggests the need for more attention to self-knowledge in the curriculum. This recommendation—in the context of good and evil—is compatible with similar suggestions now being made by scholars interested in metacognition. They, too, recommend that students learn more about their own thought processes and the affects that enhance or impede those processes. A feminine approach to moral education would include what we learn from a "morality of evil." Students not only would learn about the long history of attempts to project evil onto others but also would be helped to explore and bring to consciousness their own shadow sides. (The shadow, it should be noted, is not always evil; it contains subordinated elements that are good as well.) Self-knowledge is as important to the moral side of education as it is to the intellectual side.

Finally, programs in critical thinking—especially those that focus on social studies—should include studies that help students to understand how people are manipulated by leaders and governments into projecting evil onto other human beings called enemies. Most social studies programs today include some discussion of the injustices committed by our own government but very few explore directly and systematically the ways in which people are made into enemies. High school students learn, for example, that the Germans and Japanese were our enemies in World War II and that they are now among our allies, but they do not hear war songs like "We've got to slap the dirty little Jap," nor do they hear of General

MacArthur saying, as he wades ashore stepping over dead Japanese bodies, "That's the way I like to see them." Students thoroughly educated about their national shadow might be less likely to condemn Russians as citizens of an "evil empire" or to assume that Libyans deserve to be bombed because they follow an evil leader. The study of good and evil from a feminine perspective is essential to both personal and national wholeness.

CONCLUSION

I have made two kinds of suggestions in this chapter. On a theoretical level, I have suggested the need for phenomenologies of good and evil from the perspective of feminine experience. On the level of practice, I have suggested that an education aimed at producing good people must include feminine perspectives on good and evil. Both girls and boys need to know about the traditional association of women with evil and how religious myths have been used to maintain the subordination of women. All students need, also, to study and practice the womanly arts of caring for children, the sick, the elderly, and the needy; they need to learn how to initiate and maintain stable and gratifying relationships and how to run households in a way that nourishes bodies, minds, and spirits. They need to study the warrior model both critically and appreciatively so that its enduring virtues can be transposed to a less violent mode of living and interacting with others. Finally, they need to gain greater self-knowledge through studies that help them to accept their personal and group shadow sides. Until this material is incorporated in our school curriculum, we can hardly claim honestly that our aim is to produce good people.

Conversation as Moral Education

WHAT ROLE DOES CONVERSATION play in ethics and moral education? In this chapter, I explore a range of possible uses of conversation in moral education, beginning with its central role in discourse ethics, moving next to a brief exploration of "the immortal conversation," and finishing with a discussion of ordinary conversation and its role in moral education. Although all three forms of conversation should be of interest to moral educators, it will be argued that the last is the most important, and probably the most neglected.

FORMAL CONVERSATION

Jürgen Habermas has made conversation the centerpiece of his discourse ethics, using it in place of Kant's individual exercise of will to maintain universality. Thomas McCarthy describes Habermas's revision of the categorical imperative as follows:

> Rather than ascribing as valid to all others any maxim that I can will to be a universal law, I must submit my maxim to all others for purposes of discursively testing its claim to universality. The emphasis shifts from what each can will without contradiction to be a general law, to what all can will in agreement to be a universal norm. (1978, p. 326)

Habermas himself states the "distinctive idea of an ethics of discourse" as follows: "Only those norms can claim to be valid that meet (or could meet) with the approval of all affected in their capacity *as participants in a practical discourse*" (1983/1990, p. 66).

Participants in Habermas's conversations must have special qualities, however. They must be capable of logical reasoning, and they must be reflective enough to reject conversational moves that would destroy the process. We are not discussing ordinary conversation here, but something very like philosophical conversation.

It is not surprising, then, that Habermas looks at Kohlberg's work with considerable approval. Kohlberg's description of the development of moral reasoning gives Habermas hope that his own description of ideal conversation has some basis in reality. In an important sense, Habermas supplies the philosophical component of a competence theory, and Kohlberg (or work similar to Kohlberg's) supplies the psychological/empirical component. Habermas would prefer, of course, to use his own approach to universality and justice rather than that of Rawls, and he explicitly sets aside discussion of Kohlberg's concept of justice. The competence idea remains central. Indeed, Habermas writes approvingly of such "seminal theories" as those of Freud, Marx, Durkheim, Mead, Weber, Piaget, and Chomsky. "Each," he writes, "inserted a genuinely philosophical idea like a detonator into a particular context of research" (1983/1990, p. 15). In all of these theories, he sees a central role for philosophy: the argumentative or justificatory work underlying "empirical theories with strong universalistic claims" (p. 15).

Kohlberg's stage theory represents, for Habermas, possible documentation of the growing competence of young human beings in practical discourse. This competence, the capacity to exercise reason in moral judgment, is essential for the argumentation that Habermas puts at the center of his theory. Moral thinkers must be able to argue logically, and they must be capable of judging the force of an argument. Thus, for Habermas, Kohlberg's scheme is not just an empirical description of moral development; it really should be taken seriously as a rigorous description of competence. Habermas is attracted to the idea that a competent moral thinker at the higher levels argues and judges in the way Kohlberg has described. It is the philosopher's job to analyze the conditions under which argumentation can proceed without contradicting its own premises. It is the empirical researcher's job to show that people really do produce the moral utterances predicted by the theory. This complementarity is what Habermas finds so attractive in all the theoreticians mentioned above.

If the Habermas/Kohlberg complementarity represents a competence theory, then we have to acknowledge that the implications for moral education may be few and relatively minor. Teaching may speed up transition from one stage to another, but people should pass from one stage to the next under merely adequate stimulation. Indeed, Piaget might have dismissed our preoccupation with *teaching* moral education as the "American question." The point about education and development is made convincingly by Diana Baumrind (1993) in her response to Lawrence Walker:

If a college education is required for attainment of the higher stages, the basic premise of developmentalism is challenged. One might, of course, still argue that engagement with Kohlbergian dilemmas—if that engagement embodies real conversation—can be enormously valuable in moral education. But most of us would not depend on this device alone.

There are important objections to Habermas's discourse ethics, however, and we need to consider them. One set of objections focuses on the artificiality of conversation in Habermas's theory. Michael Walzer (1990) notes, rightly I think, that what Habermas depends on is highly idealized conversation. It is not the rough-and-tumble conversation of real people. Participants must understand that certain moves are forbidden by the very logic of argumentation. Anything that closes off debate is antithetical to the whole enterprise. Hence, competent participants do not make dogmatic assertions, put self-interest above logic, attack persons instead of arguments, or insist that personal stories carry more than a modicum of weight as evidence. Such a highly constrained conversation has little resemblance to real conversation.

There is also some concern about the number of participants required. Habermas criticizes Rawls for the monological nature of the conversation that goes on behind the veil of ignorance. Rawls himself (1971) admits that only one thinker is really necessary, because all thoroughly rational thinkers would have to agree. In contrast, Habermas rightly insists that the conversation must be pluralistic; several views may be put forward, and each may be free of obvious flaws. A competent conversational group has to assess the strength of each argument. It seems, then, that Habermas is arguing for a genuine forum—many voices dedicated to locating and accepting the argument with greatest force.

Despite Habermas's theoretical emphasis on dialogue, however, there is the legitimate question of whether his idealized conversation requires more than one speaker. The conditions of ideal speech are so constrained that we may be left with a degenerate Socratic dialogue, one in which the opposition is reduced to simple affirmation: "Indeed, Socrates; yes, that is plain; of course, Socrates" (Walzer, 1990, p. 183). Further, Habermas's frank embrace of competence theories underscores this concern. A competent moral thinker, like a competent speaker/hearer, is itself an idealized conception. There is no guarantee that competence will be reflected in any given performance of real participants in conversation.

Seyla Benhabib (1987), although largely sympathetic to the Habermasian program, also worries about the emphasis on a "generalized" other rather than a concrete other. This concern is, I think, well considered. We are not well prepared in discourse ethics to meet and respond to real people with all their needs and foibles.

Even if real conversation followed the ideal description advanced by Habermas, a serious problem would remain. Philosophical argumentation comes as close to Habermas's ideal conditions as any form of human interaction, yet agreement is rarely reached. Obvious logical errors are detected, and the arguments containing them are dismissed or revised. However, after everything is cleaned up and made logically presentable, philosophers are still hard put to decide which argument has the greatest force. Richard Bernstein (1992) comments:

> Abstractly there is something enormously attractive about Habermas's appeal to the "force of the better argument" until we ask ourselves what this means and presupposes. Even under "ideal" conditions where participants are committed to discursive argumentation, there is rarely agreement about what constitutes "the force of the better argument." We philosophers, for example, cannot even agree what are the arguments advanced in any of our canonical texts, whether Plato, Aristotle, Kant, or Hegel, etc.—and there is certainly no consensus about who has advanced the better argument. (p. 220)

Bernstein is clearly right about this but, as moral educators, we might still claim great gains if students come to recognize fallacious and weak arguments. Agreement is not ensured, but grievous error can certainly be avoided.

Another objection begins with the recognition that consensus cannot guarantee moral rightness or goodness. Certainly in a small community, people might all agree and yet be completely wrong. This could happen at a particular time in history even if every human being on earth were to give assent. People at a later time might be astonished at the moral obtuseness of previous generations. However, Habermas does not depend on the consensus of actual, concrete thinkers. His theory centers on the abstract competent moral thinker; but this focus only serves to emphasize Walzer's complaints about ideal conditions and ideal thinkers, and it aggravates our concern over how many conversational partners are actually required.

One last kind of objection should be considered. By emphasizing argumentation, Habermas may have already smuggled in a particular view of the goods to be achieved and the means by which to achieve them. Most of us have to agree with Habermas that we cannot imagine an alternative to argumentation. How can we press a view without arguing for it? Surely, at least in our culture, we cannot do other than argue for the points we wish to make. But alternatives are, in fact, emerging. Black feminist scholars have suggested that concentration on stories and the credentials of those telling the stories may be more powerful and convincing than argumentation (Collins, 1990). Philosophy today incorporates stories and personal testimony in ways unthinkable in the recent past, but even so, these stories are generally offered as illustrations or anecdotal evidence in a chain of argument. Few of us are ready to discard argument entirely. Despite this acknowledgment, it must be noted that Habermas's insistence on the centrality of argument is not quite so persuasive today as it might once have been. Beginning with argumentation, then, includes a priori some substance; the method is not purely procedural, and this casts some doubt on the claim to universality.

What should we, as moral educators, make of all this? Certainly arguments in moral philosophy should interest us. They should help us to detect weaknesses and strengths in our own positions. Also, it seems reasonable to help students learn how to conduct ideal conversation. As we do this, however, we must be careful to guard against sophistry; we do not wish to turn out students who can make the poorer case seem better and the better case seem poorer by their skill in argumentation (Carter, 1984). Another factor to be kept in mind is that competent thinkers in the moral domain may diverge in their thinking; certainly the history of moral philosophy would suggest that this is true. This observation casts some doubt on any claim that identifies a particular conception of justice—or even justice itself—as the prime characteristic of the highest level. Finally, we must remember that competence and performance are only loosely linked. When we are concerned with moving from judgment to action, we must look beyond competence theories.

CONVERSATION AS PARTICIPATION IN TRADITION

Another way to look at conversation as part of moral education involves what is sometimes referred to as the "immortal conversation." This conversation has been described and interpreted in a variety of ways. First, and perhaps most obviously, there are the religious traditions on which moral education has often depended. Of course, one difficulty with religious traditions, from the perspective of conversation, is that they are often transmitted as dogma, and conversation is reduced or converted to a special type of dialogue instruction (see Burbules, 1993, for a discussion of types of dialogue). Even Christian fundamentalists typically allow fragments of dialogue—for example, questions for clarification—in an otherwise dogmatic presentation of faith and morals (Peshkin, 1986). In these dialogues, however, conversation is severely constrained, and often certain statements and expressions are forbidden. Those who dare to utter them may be censured.

Although moral talk is often rigidly controlled in religious traditions, it is also allowed to spread over territory rarely touched by secular ethics.

Personal morality and sin are central considerations in Christian moral theory, for example, whereas secular ethics are usually more concerned with how moral agents interact with other human beings. Whatever we may feel about religious moral education, I think we must admit that it has considerable power in guiding the personal habits of young people. Adolescents who make a religious pledge to abstain from alcohol and drugs and to maintain their chastity are, perhaps, safer in a dangerous world than those who lack such clear guidelines.

Further, within the limits set by a particular tradition, conversation can be lively and inspiring. Stories can be told, exemplars studied, rituals dissected and elaborated, behavior criticized or admired. For many, such conversation is fully satisfying; for others, it falls far short. The unsatisfied want to ask dangerous questions and suggest heretical possibilities.

Character education, even when it is not explicitly religious, belongs to the same tradition. Whether the foundation is God or a cultural tradition, it is assumed that there are values to be transmitted, virtues to be encouraged, a character to be established. Much of character education grows out of the Aristotelian tradition; moral educators first seek to develop character and, as virtue is manifested, the scope of conversation is allowed to broaden. The openness of conversation varies. In the pernicious form discussed by Alice Miller (1983), there is no conversation, and the distorted "characters" that emerge are devoid of real selves. In the loving form described by Tom Lickona (1991), children are invited to express their anger, fear, and doubt.

Another form of immortal conversation comes perilously close to identifying intellectual development with moral development. I refer here to the traditional liberal arts—that set of studies long associated with the leisure class. Many writers have equated voluminous knowledge of their own culture with every form of human goodness, even moral goodness. Other, more temperate writers have defended liberal education as a privileged intellectual endeavor but have recognized that it cannot be equated with moral education. Reading John Henry Cardinal Newman (1964), for example, we are impressed by his good sense in separating the goodness of liberal knowledge from the goodness of morality, but we may well be shocked by his separation of mind and body, his insistence on the intrinsic worth of liberal knowledge and its lack of instrumental value, and his overt elitism.

When some people today deplore the loss of traditional liberal education, many of us react with some confusion. We do not think that studying the Great Books or any other canon will necessarily make our students better people, and we reject the haughtiness of those who think their knowledge is Knowledge. However, confusion arises because the questions raised in traditional liberal studies still seem central to human life. We feel that education—real education—cannot neglect the questions, Where do I stand in the world? What has my life amounted to? What might I become? (Wilshire, 1990, pp. xvii–xviii). Also, What is the meaning of life? Is there a God? What is my place in the universe? are all questions that should be explored in true education.

It is true that these questions arise and are explored in impressive ways in the great works associated with liberal education, but they may also be asked and explored in other settings. Zane Grey's cowboys ask them while riding the range under starry skies. Old ladies in their rocking chairs, shelling peas or knitting, ask them as the evening cuts off the light of a summer day. Lone fishermen standing on rocky jetties in the Atlantic twilight ask them. Moreover, studying what great thinkers have said about immortal questions is no guarantee that one will be more honest, decent, loving, or even open-minded. Without mentioning names, I can easily think of four or five superbly educated persons (all of whom deplore the condition of the American mind) who are themselves incapable of hearing or responding generously to views that differ from their own. Again we have a performance gap.

Thus I believe a grave mistake is made when we argue for the traditional liberal studies as the arena in which immortal conversations must take place. Specialization has killed much of what was liberal in liberal studies (Booth, 1988; Wilshire, 1990). But the questions remain, and teachers today should muster the courage to discuss them. Frederick Turner comments:

> So the heart of the immortality of the great conversation lies outside the conventional objects, skills, traditions, and expertise of discourse. It is not . . . merely immortality for the Great Minds; for it is precisely when these great minds give up being great minds—being experts, authorities, professionals—and become amateurs, laypersons—bullshitters, if you like—that they become immortal. Socrates and company jumped all the fences, like sophomores. (1991, p. 107)

Before leaving the discussion of this form of immortal conversation, a modification that many of us find promising should be mentioned. The use of stories in moral education—literature- or narrative-based programs—is attractive from a wide range of perspectives on moral education (see, e.g., Coles, 1989; Garrod, 1993; Tappan & Packer, 1991; Vitz, 1990). Actual curricula based on stories consider the literary quality of their stories, but most do not make the mistake of assuming that literary worth can be equated with moral worth. For all their attractiveness, these programs have a weakness; they are often confined to one discipline by the coercive structure of today's schools. Teachers of mathematics and science rarely participate in these conversations.

The third sense in which to think of immortal conversations, then, is the way suggested in Turner's remarks, and it is perhaps the most important for us as moral educators. Every school subject can be related in some way to the immortal questions. Without such relation, the subjects are mere conglomerations of skills and superficial concepts. Probing in search for these relations involves a person's "total reactions upon life," as William James put it. "To get at them" (the total reactions and attitudes), James wrote,

> you must go behind the foreground of existence and reach down to that curious sense of the whole residual cosmos as an everlasting presence, intimate or alien, terrible or amusing, lovable or odious, which in some degree every one possesses. (1902/1929, p. 35)

Too often today teachers are afraid to go behind the textbook, never mind the "foreground of existence," and we at universities do not help much with our example. We, too, are hemmed into narrow specialties, afraid of trespassing on the territories of others, and so our conversations are truncated and compartmentalized. We are embarrassed to discuss even academic ethics with our students, fearing perhaps that they will think us stuffy or old-fashioned or that they will protest at the time taken from "real" subject matter—the material they have paid to hear us profess.

Yet surely it is possible, and perhaps even morally obligatory, for us as teachers to reach that "residual cosmos." In mathematics classes, teachers can share with students the great interest of many mathematicians in theological questions: Descartes's attempt to prove God's existence, Pascal's famous wager, Newton's expressed feeling that theology is more important than mathematics, the mysticism of the Pythagoreans, the contemporary fascination of mathematicians with the infinite, mathematical arguments for a pluralistic universe and possible forms of polytheism, the Platonic positioning of mathematical forms just beneath the supreme good. Beyond all this, mathematics teachers should share relevant literature (including science fiction), poetry, games, history, and biography.

I have had a continuing discussion with a retired physics professor on the possibilities of such conversations in science classes. At first he was outraged when I suggested that both evolution and creation stories be discussed in public schools. How could a professor at a major research university suggest such a thing? Here is what I suggested: Science teachers should begin the unit on evolution by inviting students to join in the immortal conversation. How did life begin? How did human life start? How have people answered these questions? There would follow a wide-ranging discussion of creation stories from many places and times. This is a wonderful and natural opportunity for multicultural education. At this point, the physics professor relaxed a little. It would be good to tell the stories, he agreed, but surely this should not be done in *science* class. Oh, yes, I said, in science class. Next, teachers would discuss the criteria by which various kinds of stories are evaluated, and this would separate scientific stories from others. Ah, now he felt much better. But what should teachers say when students ask which story is true? I replied that teachers might then introduce some material on theories of truth and encourage students to see how complicated the issues are. Surely the science story should be presented not as true but as the one that best fits the criteria of adequacy established by current science. The physics professor liked this but now began to worry about whether teachers could do it.

And how *are* we supposed to do all this, teachers ask, when we are hard pressed to get through the required curriculum? What they do not understand when they ask this question is that one reason it is so hard to get through the standard curriculum is that we have cut it off entirely from that "residual cosmos" of which James wrote and to which Wilshire has more recently drawn our attention. Reviving attention to immortal questions should make their work easier, not harder. But even if parts of the standard curriculum have to be left out, so what? "How does the factor theorem stack up against the possible existence of God?" (Noddings, 1993, p. 6).

In concluding this section on immortal conversations, I would like to emphasize that I see value in all three interpretations. Certainly the religious traditions make an important contribution, but their conversations should be continually monitored for openness. The traditional liberal studies also contribute, and for many they provide a lifetime of rich study and reflection, but they are not the only door to the immortal conversation. I am obviously most enthusiastic about the third possibility—liberalizing each discipline from within, breaking down disciplinary barriers, and inviting students into conversations that go well beyond the narrow skills and concepts of today's school subjects.

ORDINARY CONVERSATION

This last observation brings us to what may be the very heart of moral education—the quality of ordinary conversation. Many children and adolescents lack opportunities to engage in real conversation with adults. They have brief exchanges, of course, and perhaps more than enough warnings and direct instruction: wear your heavy jacket, wipe your feet, finish your breakfast, clean your room, feed the dog, and so on (some badly neglected children do not even receive this), but I am referring to real conversation in which all parties speak, listen, and respond to one another. For many young people, this is a rare experience.

What qualities must ordinary conversation have, if it is to be valuable as moral education? First, the adult participants must be reasonably good people—people who try to be good, who consider the effects of their acts on others and respond to suffering with concern and compassion. Second, the adults must care for the children and enjoy their company. When children engage in real talk with adults who like and respect them, they are likely to emulate those adults. Even if the purpose of conversation is rarely explicit moral education, matters of moral interest will arise. Adults and children will express themselves, and opportunities for exploration, debate, and correction will arise.

Many parents and teachers make the mistake of treating children's talk as "cute," and this habit is often carried even into the teenage years. Parents listen and smile when their teenager expresses an opinion on a political or social problem. The opinion is not taken seriously, and the adults do not press the child for evidence, point out feasible alternatives, express their own views seriously, or confess their own confusion. In other words, these parents do not really converse with their children, and the children do not learn to listen attentively or to construct persuasive arguments.

Perhaps most significantly of all, in ordinary conversation, we are aware that our partners in conversation are more important than the topic. Participants are not trying to win a debate; they are not in a contest with an opponent. They are conversing because they like each other and want to be together. The moment is precious in itself. The content of the conversation, the topic, may or may not become important. Sometimes it does, and the conversation becomes overtly educational and memorable on that account. At other times, the only memory that lingers is one of warmth and laughter or sympathy and support (Noddings, 1991).

This essential feature of one type of ordinary conversation—that the partner is more important than the topic—can be used as a lens to examine the other forms of conversation we have discussed. When children are invited to discuss moral dilemmas, for example, we want to be sure that their conversations remain respectful of other participants. Participants can engage in a constructive and mutual search for the truth or they can engage in eristic and aim to defeat their opponents. We do not have to give up our search for a better way or for something like truth (even if we cannot define either perfectly) when we place our conversational partners above all else.

However, this is tricky. When we examine typical (or stereotypical) male conversation—traditional ethics, and indeed most professional domains constructed by men—we usually find a tremendous emphasis on the search for truth. Arguments may become heated and even ruthless; opponents may be devastated in the name of truth. When we examine a typical (or stereotypical) female conversation, we often find a softening of language, a willingness to withdraw in order not to hurt. The conversation may be sprinkled with digressions, apparent non sequiturs and much beating about the bush. Both stereotypes or extremes should probably be avoided. It can be hard work to make conflict constructive, and conversations of the sort that keep concern for one's partner paramount and still seek the better way are usually voluntary conversations between people who have some affection for each other. They always require trust, if not affection.

That may be the key and the reason that ordinary conversation of a certain kind is so valuable in moral education. When people have loving regard for one another, they can engage in constructive conflict—although it is by no means easy even then. But when people dislike or distrust one another, what then? Here is where we should lean, I think, toward the female extreme. To establish a relation in which people may come to have positive regard for one another, we need to engage in conversation about shared interests and everyday events. We must stay away from the direct object of inquiry. I am not alone in making such a suggestion. John Dewey advised long ago that we should not start politics with political issues if we want to solve a problem, and, more recently, Harold Saunders (1991) has given similar advice on diplomatic disputes. Today we may well learn more about the value and the strategies of such conversations by studying the "different voice" as it speaks in sensitive interactions.

Once a relation is established, when it has become unthinkable to do violence to this other with whom we disagree, we may be able to address the conflict itself. A compromise may be reached. The force of the better argument may be acknowledged. Nevertheless, sometimes there will be no resolution. The parties will remain solidly in their original thought-camps. However, if they maintain their regard or just remain pledged to do each other no harm, a great moral victory has been won.

The kind of ordinary conversation described above is, among other things, preparation for a constructive approach to conflict. The description is not morally neutral, and I claim no universality for it. It leaves open the definition of goodness and suggests a wide range of acceptable views. Insistence on respect and loving regard leaves us open to influence; we are pledged to learning and exploring together, not to a total transmission of moral values. Finally, putting our partners above our arguments and principles suggests limits on what we will do to win our points or enact our principles. This is preparation for a moral life of openness, friendliness, trust, and caring. It is preparation that takes time. It requires constancy from the adult participants.

We live in a time when everyone seems to be looking for quick and sure solutions. Computer companies have even begun to advertise ways in which computers can replace parents. They are too late—television has already done that. Seriously, however, in every branch of education, including moral education, we make a mistake when we suppose that a particular batch of content or a particular teaching method or a particular configuration of students and space will accomplish our ends. The answer is both harder and simpler. We, parents and teachers, have to live with our children, talk to them, listen to them, enjoy their company, and show them by what we do and how we talk that it is possible to live appreciatively or, at least, nonviolently with most other people. After all, there is no guarantee that a person who has been reasonably good for 40 or 70 years will finish his or her life as a good person. Tragedy does strange and terrible things to us (Nussbaum, 1986). We can supplement ordinary conversation with healthy religious instruction, with powerful and sensitive intellectual training, with all sorts of commonsense parenting techniques, and we still cannot demand guarantees. Instead we must place our bets somewhere and remain in relations of care and trust with our children. We must have faith in the outcome.

I have described a kind of ordinary conversation between adults and children that is central to moral education. It has at least three important characteristics:

1. The adults are people who try to be good, even if they do not always bring it off.
2. The adults have loving regard and respect for their child partners.
3. For both parties, in the conversation under consideration, the partner is more important than the topic, the conclusion, or the argument.

In such conversations, children learn all sorts of things—facts, the rules of polite conversation, manner and style, trust and confidence, how to listen, how to respond without hurting, and a host of other factors in human interaction. Because parents are so harried today and because so many do not fit the criteria I have suggested, teachers simply must engage their students in ordinary conversation. The kind of people we are turning out is far more important than national supremacy in mathematics and science. Teachers must be free to "jump all the fences" and explore matters of great and small importance with their students.

We moral educators can also profit from a consideration of conversation in our own interactions. As our attention shifts from judgment to action, from justification to motivation, we should find some intelligent use for the core insights that have been developed in several competing models of moral education. That means engaging in constructive formal, immortal, and ordinary conversations ourselves.

Stories and Conversation in Schools

MANY PEOPLE TODAY are deeply concerned about the apparent decline in moral standards among young people. Sharing the concern but beleaguered by demands for higher academic standards, educators wonder what role they can and should play in moral education. If we accept the premise that education by its very nature has a moral dimension, there is no question that educators must play a role in moral education. It is reasonable to ask whether academic and moral goals might be approached together in such a way that both are more likely to be attained. As we consider this important educational task, it will be clear that genuine moral education requires the construction of shared meanings, not simply the processing of information.

In an earlier chapter, I described three forms of conversation that can be useful in moral education. In this chapter, I will consider ways in which these three forms can be used in connection with stories. The discussion will focus on secondary education for two reasons: First, stories have always been a large part of the best elementary education, and several fine literature-based programs in moral education are already in use. Second, secondary schools today are almost universally described as "boring"; many are also described as dangerous and nasty places, so the need to do something in the line of moral education is especially pressing at that level. A program that includes stories can perhaps combat the complaint of boredom, increase moral sensitivity, and add to cultural literacy.

THREE FORMS OF CONVERSATION

Forms of conversation that have an obvious place in schools include the formal conversation typical of scholarly debate and discourse ethics, talk (formal or informal) centered on topics often included in the "immortal conversation," and the ordinary conversation of everyday life. Oddly, although all three are appropriate in education, none of them appears regularly in secondary schools. Far more frequently, we see the typical pattern of teacher elicitation, student response, teacher evaluation (Mehan, 1979). Even in teachers' lectures, we rarely hear what might be called a conversational style—that is, a presentation that includes stories, controversial comments, and statements of puzzlement and wonder, one that is clearly intended to invite eventual conversation.

Formal conversation is perhaps best captured in philosophy, where it is conducted more often in writing than in oral discussion. It is characterized by a "serious" content—something at issue, a problematic matter to be settled—and by a set of widely recognized procedural rules. People engaged in such conversations agree (at least tacitly) to a number of conventions, among them to take turns speaking, to address the issue and not to attack their partners in conversation, to define new terms as they are introduced, to tell the truth, to give credit to others for words or ideas deliberately borrowed, to use universally accepted rules of logic, and to accept the force of the better argument in coming to conclusions. When this form is discussed in the next section, we will see that opportunities for such conversations arise in all parts of the curriculum. We will see also that, when competent thinkers engage in this form of conversation, a grasp of "the facts"—even agreement on facts—is insufficient to settle most controversial issues. Interpretation of the facts is crucial.

Talk that can be described as part of the "immortal conversation" might fall into this pattern, but it might also be more like everyday conversation. Questions about the origin of the universe and the meaning of life, death, suffering, and goodness are asked not only by philosophers but, as we saw in the last chapter, also by people in every walk of life. Again, although the opportunities are numerous, actual participation in the immortal conversation is rare in secondary schools.

Even everyday conversation is rare between teachers and students. Everything is businesslike. Teachers teach, and students either do what they are told or resist. In neither case does conversation usually occur. Yet kids long for conversation with adults. In *Voices from the Inside* (Institute for Education in Transformation, 1992), one high school student says:

> Teachers should get to know their students a little better, not to where they bowl together but at least know if they have any brothers or sisters. I have found that if I know my teacher I feel more obliged to do the work so I don't disappoint them. Once my trust is gained I feel I should work for myself and also for the teacher. (p. 21)

When students are recognized in conversation, they often respond with touching gratitude. Another student remarks:

My teacher shows an honest concern about how we feel. He'll give us time to let our emotions out instead of just work, work, work. Like, for example, today he asked how I felt about the Rodney King trial. That's something I needed to release. I've walked around all day with a frown until my feeling was expressed. Thanx 2 him. (p. 19)

Statements like these should help to convince educators that ordinary conversation with students should not always be considered time "off-task" or time wasted. As the first student's words so poignantly show, time in conversation often means trust gained, and trust gained means that the teacher acquires a partner in the effort to educate.

In the next three sections, we will look more deeply into the three forms of conversation and the kinds of stories that might be used to initiate or enhance them.

FORMAL CONVERSATION

Some of the conventions of formal conversation are well taught in schools, for example, turn-taking (Hansen, 1993) and not attacking one's opponent personally. Other aspects are less well treated. The greatest deficiency, of course, is the lack of conversation itself. But even preparation for formal conversation is widely neglected. It is not unusual to find students in good graduate schools who have not been exposed to the elements of logic that are assumed in formal conversation, and many are reluctant to evaluate the force of the better argument, preferring instead to adopt a politically correct position and defend it emotionally. Others prefer to give back their teachers' words in the simplest form of information processing. Both groups—those who employ emotional rhetoric and those who want only an exchange of facts—are unable to engage adequately in formal conversation.

It is important to understand that I will not argue that training in logic will automatically increase attention to formal conversation (it may even have the opposite effect), nor will I argue that such training will necessarily have beneficial transfer effects in mathematics or any other subject. Typically, educators ask for too much assurance along these lines before they risk experimenting with promising approaches.

I will make the following claims for teaching basic logic: Teaching basic logic in mathematics classes gives teachers opportunities to talk about matters that have relevance well beyond mathematics, yet are not irrelevant to mathematics. Basic training in logic may encourage students to examine all sorts of arguments for logical validity and thus enhance the quest for meaning. Exposure to logic may open a fascinating field of recreation for some students. Finally, such exposure can broaden cultural literacy.

In my years as a high school mathematics teacher, I included a unit on logic in many of my classes, and now in graduate courses in philosophy of education, I still find such a unit useful. Consider what can be done with material from *Alice in Wonderland* (M. Gardner, 1963). The book is so rich in logical, historical, linguistic, and philosophical material that I cannot do it justice here, but let's examine one scene. Alice has stopped to ask directions from the Cheshire Cat and is told that whatever direction she chooses, she'll encounter someone who is mad. The following conversation takes place:

> "But, I don't want to go among mad people," Alice remarked.
> "Oh, you can't help that," said the Cat: "we're all mad here. I'm mad. You're mad."
> "How do you know I'm mad?" said Alice.
> "You must be," said the Cat, "or you wouldn't have come here."
> Alice didn't think that proved it at all: however, she went on: "And how do you know you're mad?"
> "To begin with," said the Cat, "a dog's not mad. You grant that?"
> "I suppose so," said Alice.
> "Well, then," the Cat went on, "you see a dog growls when it's angry, and wags its tail when it's pleased. Now I growl when I'm pleased, and wag my tail when I'm angry. Therefore, I'm mad." (p. 89)

I usually ask students to discuss both parts of the Cat's argument. Under what premises is the first part of the argument valid (that Alice must be mad)? Why is the second argument invalid even if we grant the premises (that a dog's not mad, that it growls when angry, etc.)? A careful examination of the two arguments gives us an opportunity to talk about the differences between truth and validity and to employ some of the skills that should be developed before tackling this exercise. I usually give students experience with basic truth tables for atomic sentences including negations, converses, inverses, and contrapositives. They also know the basic syllogistic form or law of detachment. Most eventually unravel the second argument and decide that the Cat has only "proved" that a cat is not a dog, not that cats must be mad.

But beyond the basic logic, which may prove useful in both mathematics and everyday life, the topic may be expanded in many directions. At the beginning of their conversation, the Cat tells Alice that, in one direction, there lives a "Mad Hatter." Where did such an expression come from? It turns out that before the dangers of mercury were known, hatters often did go mad. Mercury was used in curing felt, and hatters often exhibited the signs of mercury poisoning: shaking, addled speech, hallucinations, and other psychotic symptoms (M. Gardner, 1963, p. 90). Is there reason today, then, to be concerned about mercury in fish and other food products? How much contaminated tuna fish (and at what level of contamination) would we have to eat to be afflicted with "hatter's shakes"?

Besides looking at the etymology of terms and the direct use of logic, we might induce an interest in biography. In recent years, there has been increased interest in the life and times of Charles Dodgson (Lewis Carroll) (Cohen, 1995). Was his interest in little girls innocent? What contributions did he make to logic proper? What events in his life contributed to his shyness? Why have Freudians been so interested in *Alice*? (And what *is* a Freudian?) These questions illustrate the possibilities for widening conversation in secondary school classrooms. Students are encouraged to think beyond the mere algorithms of logic and processing of information.

The effort to use *Alice* for educational purposes might also lead to poking a little fun at ourselves, and students will surely enjoy that diversion. G.K. Chesterton understood the teacher's mind. He wrote:

> Poor, poor, little Alice! She has not only been caught and made to do lessons; she has been forced to inflict lessons on others. Alice is now not only a school girl but a school mistress. The holiday is over and Dodgson is again a don. There will be lots and lots of examination papers, with questions like: (1) What do you know about the following: mimsy, gimble, haddocks' eyes, treacle-wells, beautiful soup? (2) Record all the moves in the chess game in *Through the Looking-Glass*, and give diagrams. (3) Outline the practical policy of the White Knight for dealing with the social problem of green whiskers. (4) Distinguish between Tweedledum and Tweedledee. (quoted in M. Gardner, 1963, n.p.)

Chesterton is right, of course. The teaching mind too often gets bogged down in information processing and retelling on tests. But we need not make our questions into examination questions; rather, we can make them into topics of conversation, and the topics of conversation may focus on almost any academic discipline or on a host of everyday interests.

Philosophers often use stories called philosophical fictions to challenge the theoretical positions of other philosophers. The scenarios are designed to illustrate an unhappy effect of a particular position or a contingency that cannot be handled easily from that perspective. Then a philosopher defending the initial position has to show how the unhappy effect can be blocked or how the contingency can be met. Such work is far more demanding than simply collecting and organizing information.

Fascinating as this work is, it does not have the multifaceted power of literary stories. In addition to providing exercise in logical applications, stories borrowed from real literature reach beyond the purpose at hand and enhance cultural literacy, make connections to other disciplines, and offer intrinsic value. They are in themselves worth talking about.

There is another reason why teachers today might be interested in promoting the skills required by formal conversation. These skills are necessary for civil public life. Indeed, as we saw earlier, Jürgen Habermas (1990) has placed conversation at the center of ethics. The idea is that people, following the rules of formal conversation, must communicate with one another and come to agreement on the norms that will govern their lives. "Only those norms can claim to be valid that meet (or could meet) with the approval of all affected in their capacity *as participants in a practical discourse*" (Habermas, 1983/1990, p. 66). Students can be given practice in such discourse through class meetings and similar strategies. Opportunities to engage in formal conversation about the rules that govern their own classroom lives should help to convince students that there are political and social uses for this form of conversation.

We should not, however, exaggerate the usefulness of formal conversation. History is liberally sprinkled with examples of highly trained people who knew the conventions of formal conversation and quickly cast them aside in the heat of emotional debate. Political debate is rife with ad hominem attacks, non sequiturs, and other gross violations of the rules. Scientific debate has not been without its emotional clashes, nor has philosophical discourse. Further, philosophical debate reveals a difficulty that may be impossible to overcome. Even the best-trained people find it hard to judge which are the best arguments. Recall Richard Bernstein's comments on this difficulty. Difficulties such as these have to be faced squarely. Consensus is not always possible, and many postmodern thinkers advise that it is often not even desirable. Basic differences between individuals and groups must be recognized and, if they are not morally reprehensible, respected (Derrida, 1978). But the fact that consensus is often either unlikely or undesirable does not imply that we should abandon norms of civility and logical debate. It means, rather, that we need more than procedural conventions to guide our lives, and that observation brings us to the next form of conversation.

THE IMMORTAL CONVERSATION

Since humans have been capable of conversation, they have engaged in the "immortal conversation." In this conversation, we are more deeply concerned with the content than with the process. Matters of birth, death, cruelty, pain, misfortune, love, good fortune—all the topics central to fairy tales, legends, and religions—are of interest to people everywhere, and they get far too little attention in schools obsessed with short answers and the accumulation of information.

Let us consider an example. Among the matters that arise perennially are all the questions about origins and creation. Universal interest in these questions suggests that science teachers might do well to discuss creation stories with their students. Not only should a wide range of creation stories be told but so should the stories of the debates involving these stories. Instead of hiding the debates behind school board meeting doors, the debates should be an exciting part of the curriculum—an opportunity to learn the skills of formal conversation and an initiation into the "immortal conversation."

Students should hear about the highly emotional exchanges between Bishop Wilberforce and T. H. Huxley, Darwin's doubts about a loving creator in the wake of the natural horrors he observed, the Scopes trial, and present-day arguments over evolution and creation. They should be introduced to literature and poetry that include explorations of these issues (Noddings, 1993), and they should be invited to join that great conversation. They should hear, too, some of the humor on the subject. Here, for example, is a comment from Stephen Leacock (1956) on how things proceeded after the start:

> Once started, the nebulous world condensed into suns, the suns threw off planets, the planets cooled, life resulted and presently became conscious, conscious life got higher up and higher up till you had apes, then Bishop Wilberforce, and then Professor Huxley. (p. 2463)

There are many other topics in the great conversation. Another of special importance to high school students centers on the good life. What constitutes a good life? Teachers might note that, at least from the time of Aristotle, thoughtful people have discussed two aspects of the good life: the material conditions, or "goods," required and the personal development characteristic of a good life. *Having* goods and *being* good are both part of the good life and interact to enhance each other.

It is widely observed today—and hard to challenge—that we live in a highly materialistic society. Material goods seem to define the good life almost entirely for many people. It might be good for high school students to hear about people who lacked these goods and nevertheless possessed, or at least strove for, other goods. The object here is not to minimize the suffering and deprivation of our present students but to arouse in them both pity and admiration for the many, many generations of people who struggled and suffered with far less hope of achieving either material goods or personal recognition. Again, the object is not simply to provide students with more information, although the expanded conversation will certainly do that. Instead, the object is to arouse sensibilities, to get students to think and feel beyond the facts, to reach for what all this means for their own lives and the lives of others.

The teaching of literature provides a wonderful opportunity for the discussion of moral sentiments. Even if there is insufficient time for a high school class to read all of Dickens's *Bleak House*, teachers might combine telling and reading to convey the multitude of life stories dramatized by Dickens. Portraits are painted vividly: of faith, constancy, unselfishness, greediness, shiftiness, cruelty, cleverness, shame, regret, pompousness, and "rising above it all." Excerpts should be read to convey the life of Jo—a boy growing up without home or family. Dickens (1853), simultaneously mocking the "good" ladies whose efforts are directed to faraway places and hoping to shame his fellow citizens into doing something to relieve the misery on their doorsteps, describes Jo:

> He is not one of Mrs. Pardiggle's Tockahoopo Indians; he is not one of Mrs. Jellyby's lambs, . . . he is not softened by distance and unfamiliarity; he is not a genuine foreign-grown savage; he is the ordinary home-made article. Dirty, ugly, disagreeable to all the senses, in body a common creature of the common streets, only in soul a heathen. Homely filthe begrimes him, homely parasites devour him, homely sores are in him, homely rags are on him; native ignorance, the growth of English soil and climate, sinks his immortal nature lower than the beasts that perish. (p. 259)

Yet, when he is questioned and charged to tell the truth about an event he witnessed, Jo responds:

> "Wisher may die if I don't, sir," says Jo, reverting to his favorite declaration. "I never done anythink yit, but wot you knows on, to get myself into no trouble. I never was in no other trouble at all, sir—'sept not knowin' nothink and starwation." (p. 259)

One cannot argue that Jo, who dies shortly after this exchange, lived the "good life" merely because he had a basic desire to be good. He lacked entirely the material resources for a good life and lived one of lonely misery. The story should induce pity, indignation, and humility. Cultural literacy and human feeling need not be mutually exclusive.

So often, even in English classes, opportunities to engage in the "immortal conversation" are ignored in favor of teaching material or literary facts and techniques. But one can admire the literary mastery of Dickens without neglecting the great human stories in his work. *Bleak House* presents a panorama of characters who are personifications of human attributes. Scarcely any real human being could be as greedy and nasty as old Mr. Smallweed, as cheerfully parasitic as Skimpole, as deluded and lost as Richard, as steady and decent as Mr. Jarndyce, as obtuse and self-righteous as Mrs. Jellyby, as wise and selfless as Esther, as crafty and just as Mr. Bucket, as egotistical and stupid as Mr. Guppy. Yet all of these characters ring true, and we learn from them. By contrasting Jarndyce and Richard, we see that desire for more wealth—especially contingent and un-earned wealth—can actually weaken and even destroy happiness. Jarndyce resolutely refuses to think about a possible legacy that is under litigation and lives a contented life; Richard pins all his hopes on the possibility and thereby loses every chance at happiness.

In every school subject, it is possible to introduce discussion of the good life and what it might consist in. Students might well be deeply touched by the story of Josie told by W. E. B. Du Bois (1989). Already 20 years old when she met Du Bois, who was hired to teach in her poor community, "she herself longed to learn" (p. 44). What happened to Josie? For a while at least she came to school with her younger brothers and sisters, and Du Bois loved visiting her and her family:

> Best of all I loved to go to Josie's, and sit on the porch, eating peaches, while the mother hustled and talked: how Josie had bought the sewing-machine; how Josie worked at service in winter, but that four dollars a month was "mighty little" wages; how Josie longed to go away to school, but that it "looked like" they never would get far enough ahead to let her. (pp. 47–48)

Du Bois taught for two years in Josie's community, and then left to further his own education. In that short time, Josie's appetite was "whet-ted . . . by school and story and half-awakened thought." But what came of this appetite, this awakening? Du Bois returned ten years later:

> Josie was dead, and the gray-haired mother said simply, "we've had a heap of trouble since you've been away."

Through all this time, Josie had worked for her family—worked and scraped. Then one year when the spring came,

> and the birds twittered, and the stream ran proud and full, little sister Lizzie, bold and thoughtless, flushed with the passion of youth, bestowed herself on the tempter, and brought home a nameless child. Josie shivered and worked on, with the vision of schooldays all fled, with a face worn and tired,—worked until, on a summer's day, someone married another; then Josie crept to her mother like a hurt child, and slept—and sleeps. (p. 50)

It is hard to read this account even now, separated by time and space, without crying. How many lives, potentially so rich, have been lost? Might such stories increase the resolve of students to do something with their own lives? Again, one can see that students may react to this story in a variety of ways. As teachers, we are not trying to get students to memorize paragraphs from Du Bois or to answer short questions about life in Appalachia. We want them *to think*, and if some decide—like Scarlett O'Hara—that they will never go hungry or lack material resources, we should be ready with stories that prompt still deeper thought.

Besides material resources, human beings need projects, forms of work that they can embrace wholeheartedly. Mathematics teachers might tell the story of the great mathematician James Sylvester, who had to overcome the overt prejudice against Jews in British academic establishments. Still, mathematics was the great project at the center of his life. Of it, he said:

> There is no study in the world which brings into more harmonious action all the faculties of the mind than [mathematics] . . . the mathematician lives long and lives young; the wings of the soul do not early drop off, nor do its pores become clogged with the earthy particles blown from the dusty highways of vulgar life. (quoted in Bell, 1937/1965, p. 405)

Sylvester's language is a bit flowery for our times, but the message and its enthusiasm are clear. Sylvester himself lived a long life, productive to the end, and remained enthusiastic not only about mathematics but about music and poetry. Teachers can find similar stories about musicians, artists, farmers, nurses, naturalists, priests, and—yes—teachers.

In addition to material resources and projects, the good life according to Aristotle—and few of us would disagree—requires friends. Friends (Aristotle contended) not only provide companionship in shared recreations, they also encourage us to be the best persons we can be. Students should be invited to look at friendship this way. Again, good literature abounds in stories that illustrate this feature of Aristotelian friendship (and also the many failures of friends to understand and support one another).

If teachers and curriculum makers thought first in terms of themes such as the good life and its components and second about the literature to be selected, high school education might gain in coherence as well as relevance. For example, in choosing literature on the friendship theme, we might think of *A Separate Peace* (Knowles, 1959), which is usually in the curriculum anyway, but tied into the theme, it would have special significance. The friendship of Gene and Finny is flawed by Gene's competitiveness and the projection of his own rivalry onto Finny. Teachers can move in many directions with the ideas found here. They can explore rivalry and competitiveness. When is it healthy and when not? What is its relation to enmity and war? What is the school's role in producing and maintaining rivalries? Sticking close to the theme of friendship, however, they might want to concentrate on what friends mean to one another, the nature of respect, the need for openness, the obligation to protect, the gift of forgiveness, and the guilt suffered when friends hurt one another.

When a theme has been chosen, it is logical to ask what other works might be read that illustrate the theme. That question is very different from the more general and academic question, What else (from the canon, for example) should they read? Instead, given the theme of friendship, we ask, Where do interesting friendships appear? Teachers might think of the friendship between Huck and the slave Jim in *Huckleberry Finn*. This friendship is an anomalous one—even illegal. What makes it a friendship? Discussion of anomalous friendships might lead to consideration of Steinbeck's *Of Mice and Men*, in which the friendship between Lenny and George illustrates another kind of friendship across difference.[1] Mary Gordon's *The Company of Women* (1980) describes a beautiful lifelong friendship among women, and it also introduces the dilemma of "particular friendships" and the proscription against them for members of the Catholic priesthood and orders. Was Cyprian, the priest in Gordon's story, a failure because he needed and welcomed the warmth of particular human beings? Near death, Cyprian blames himself for his priestly failure but also looks longingly and appreciatively on his human connections. He confesses:

> I think it is unbearable that one day I will not see their faces. I fear the moment of death when one longs only for a human face, that beat, that second between death and life eternal when there is nothing, and for a moment one is utterly alone before entering the terrible, beautiful room of judgment. (Gordon, 1980, p. 287)

In planning for such a thematic unit, one need not ignore current literary crazes. Jane Austen's *Pride and Prejudice* yields two lovely friendships for discussion: one between the sisters Jane and Elizabeth (can sisters be friends?) and the other between Bingley and Darcy. In the latter, was it right for Darcy to protect Bingley from what he (Darcy) mistakenly judged to be an inappropriate or potentially painful relationship?

Throughout this section, I have concentrated on stories that have direct academic relevance and a high level of intellectual respectability, but, of course, teachers might add stories from teenage literature, television dramas, news, sports, or any other source, and some of these possibilities will be addressed in the final section on ordinary conversation. My point has been to show that we can enhance intellectual literacy (if we want to do so) without sacrificing what is more universally important—understanding the existential condition and, in particular, moral life.

ORDINARY CONVERSATION

The three types of conversation are not discrete; they run into one another, and one cannot always tell when the conversational switch has occurred. For example, a group might be involved in discussing friendship as a necessary component of the good life. An example, say, Elizabeth and Jane in *Pride and Prejudice*, might lead to discussion of the movie, and some students might begin talking about other movies they have seen recently, with whom they attend shows, what they eat before, during, and after shows. It has always been a problem for teachers to decide when to bring the class back to the topic and when to let the conversation run on. Teachers often feel intuitively that these digressions are somehow important, but they do not know exactly why, and they feel guilty—sometimes "used" or "had"— when students effectively steer the conversation away from the initial subject matter.

Let me try to defend the intuitive notion that these conversations can be important. Both teachers and students often feel closer to life's core during these conversations, but the emphasis on information processing and accumulation of facts give such conversation an illicit appearance. Here, again, cultural literacy and existential exploration need not be at odds. As students talk, teachers come to know them better. As teachers join the conversation, students get glimpses of the teacher as a human being. Recall the longing expressed by the student in *Voices from the Inside* (Institute for Education in Transition, 1992). Kids want to know their teachers better, and when they do, they "feel obliged" to work not only for themselves but for the teacher, whom they now trust. In today's large schools and fragmented communities, trust is not easily established. Students and teachers rarely meet each other in the market, church, or community gathering, and the relationship between them has become more and more professional— professional in the sense of marked status difference, detachment, and goal orientation.

As students and teachers slip into ordinary conversation, they learn about one another. But they also learn *from* one another. Without imposing their values, teachers can convey all sorts of messages about respect, taste, choice, time management, humor, human foibles, fears, disappointments. It is hard to exaggerate how much it might mean to a particular student to hear a teacher say, "That happened to me once too." And sometimes students disclose things about themselves that change the opinion of a teacher drastically.

I recall talking to a general mathematics class years ago about their participation in nighttime demonstrations. This was during the time of racial disturbances back in the sixties. I told the kids frankly that I was afraid someone would get hurt. My remarks opened a conversation that threatened to become explosive. White boys in the class bragged that they "were ready"—armed to the teeth, if one could believe them. Black boys laughed and scoffed. They were already engaged in "busting heads" and committing all sorts of mayhem—if one could believe *them*. Then the White boys described their guns, and one tough guy challenged the most outspoken Black boy to describe his gun. "I don't have one," he replied. "Oh, come on," urged the White boy, "how about your hunting gun?" "I don't hunt," James blurted out, "I've always been afraid of hurting someone." Dead silence followed this admission. The threat was over. And the relationship between James and me was ever after one of mutual appreciation. His name was not "James," but I remember his real name, and details of his difficult life stay with me. I no longer remember the White boy's name.

My story of one ordinary conversation is unique in its details, as all stories are, but its form and effects are repeated elsewhere. Lee Colsant (1995) recounts a series of such stories in the tale of his transformation as a teacher. Attempting to teach French culture to inner-city Chicago kids in the same way that he had successfully taught kids in Quebec, Colsant finds himself sliding into despair. In an account that is touchingly honest, Colsant admits that he comes to hate his first-period class. The kids despise him, and he despises them. But then he decides to make peace and start over. He listens; he reasons openly with them about their mutual problem; he tries group work.

The initial result is a melange of voices, messages, resolutions, and debacles. Colsant admits:

> I try to acknowledge my failure and their resistance while giving them a choice, even an invitation to join and work. Instead, I make them feel they are outsiders, wrong if they don't join the rest. I am still pushing French on them. My old self speaks while I try to find my new voice. The dilemma is not resolved. I am not making it. (p. 69)

But Colsant does make it. He does not ever teach French in the way he once taught it, but he connects with kids who need the trust, respect, and example of an adult who cares for them, and he does teach some French, albeit a far different one from the old standard curriculum. From him, the kids learn something about cooperation, polite modes of exchange, persistence, and concern for the feelings of others. They begin to use French expressions to convey short messages. From them, Colsant learns what it means to live life on the border—no security of place, no recognition, no security, even for one's life. And, of course, in the end, Colsant suffers a loss when students move away suddenly, leaving unanswered the tacit questions, Why? to Where? with Whom? The loss is even greater when a student or former student is shot dead. Suffering is one of the costs of relating. Thinking back on the student who moved (where?) and the one who died, Colsant knows the debt he owes them—what he learned from them. He sees them in his new students:

> New lads are there all right, not remote antagonists, but alive in the toil of listening. New conversations will surely emerge. (p. 89)

Conversations reveal care, promote trust, and invite remembrance. Colsant's kids began to repeat his often-used response, "I don't know; think it through." They may use it with their own children someday. Sloganlike expressions that emerge either in conversations or in routines can reverberate years later in the memory of students. Philip Jackson (1992) recalls a favorite teacher and how her slogan, "Keep your wits about you," recurs in his reflective thinking. And he reminds us of something especially relevant to the present discussion. He says, "I think it would be hard to say which came first, my liking for Mrs. Henzi or my successful mastery of the material she taught" (p. 4). Whether that liking comes through masterfully run routines, personal kindness, or spontaneous conversation, it is something too often overlooked in the study and practice of teaching. It matters whether or not students like their teachers and teachers like their students. It matters to the teachers, and it matters to the students. "I feel more obliged." "I don't want to disappoint them." This could be a teacher's voice as easily as a student's.

Ordinary conversations, if they are more than mere banter, provide opportunities for telling personal stories. Students get to reveal something of themselves (whether, for example, they have brothers and sisters), and teachers become real persons. The latter may be especially important for students who have no other models of educated persons in their lives. Uneducated parents, no matter how much they love their children, cannot provide such models. To be effective as models, however, teachers have to be real people, people whose life experiences, desires, and disappointments seem real and lead students to believe that they can also become educated persons—without becoming alien creatures.

Legitimate questions arise about the length and scope of ordinary conversations in the classroom. Teachers who have achieved a high level of artistry seem able to bring even the most esoteric conversations back to the initial topic at just the right time. How do they do this? How do great violinists and cellists produce the effects that set them apart from run-of-the-mill musicians? Practice, sensitivity, and a great love for what they are doing seem paramount. In teaching, a wide repertoire of stories, careful planning, and passionate interest seem vital. As David Hawkins (1973) pointed out years ago, one has to *plan* for spontaneity.

Planning might be thought of in two ways: planning for the upcoming lesson and preparing more generally for one's future teaching. Both senses of planning have been handled badly in teacher education and supervision. Teachers are encouraged (coerced?) by supervision in schools to plan skimpily—learning objectives, page numbers, and assignments crammed into small spaces. This is another horrible example of the overemphasis on mere facts. In contrast, a teacher-artist plans far more extensively. A mathematics teacher, for example, may work all of the problems he or she plans to assign, carefully noting places where alternative methods are possible, places where mistakes are likely, prerequisite skills for certain moves, interesting shortcuts, interesting numbers, interesting mathematicians who spring to mind as the interesting numbers are considered. The planning may involve charts and diagrams, but it is, in its entirety, more like a growing web or even a stellar explosion than a flow chart. Such planning is deeply satisfying in itself and is directed at both the immediate lesson and future lessons. Much that appears in this kind of planning is not actually used in the lesson that instigates it. Rather, it becomes material for possible conversations and contributes to the growth of the teacher. Indeed, we might say that it enriches the teacher's internal conversation. Further, teachers who plan this way are perpetually alive to all the possibilities around them that might contribute to their classroom virtuosity.

Teachers with this sort of mastery have little need for the mechanistic forms of control so popular today. Like other artists, they have control of the artistic medium. They know where most conversations might go, and they are prepared to change course when a change seems appropriate. They can take risks because they know that they will be able to handle most of the problems likely to arise.

I have been arguing that ordinary conversations in classrooms are important in themselves. Their occurrence *in a rich learning environment* is a sign that relationships of care and trust are being established. I have emphasized the phrase "in a rich learning environment" because I do not mean to suggest that ordinary conversation should fill the entire school day. There clearly must be time for the practice of technical skills, direct instruction, formal conversation, and the semifocused conversation that we call the "immortal conversation" among other familiar school activities. Students themselves are often the best judges of balance among activities. When teachers use conversation—banter—to cover for lack of preparation and when that conversation goes nowhere and creates no need to think or evaluate, students lose interest in it, and they lose respect for such teachers.

It may be especially important today for teachers to participate in conversations with their students because conversation in homes seems to have diminished. Working parents, tight schedules, and television have all contributed to the reduction in conversation. In a rich learning environment, however, students regard ordinary conversations as a mark of respect. In such conversations, as we noted before, students learn all sorts of things—facts, the rules of polite conversation, manner and style, trust and confidence, how to listen, how to respond without hurting one another, and a host of other things. These conversations are essential to moral life. They are part of moral education because when they are properly conducted, we learn through them how to meet and treat one another. They are part of moral life because such exchanges with other people are essential to the good life.

CONCLUSION

I have argued that conversation should play a much larger role in classrooms than it does today, and I have tried to show how stories can be used in these conversations. Sometimes the stories provide starting points for conversation, and sometimes conversations provide the setting in which stories emerge. Guided by a sensitive and well-prepared teacher, these stories and conversations have the potential to contribute significantly to moral life and education.

Three kinds of conversation were discussed: formal conversation—the sort of serious, rule-bound conversation characteristic of philosophy; the "immortal conversation," which may be formal or informal but is distinguished by its subject matter—the great existential questions; and ordinary conversation—the sort in which friends and acquaintances regularly engage. All these forms are likely to increase engagement, enhance cultural literacy, and contribute to the construction of relations of care and trust. An education rich in conversation clearly goes well beyond information processing and the accumulation of facts. It addresses matters central to life itself.

NOTE

1. For other examples of friendships across difference, see A. J. Cronin, *The Keys of the Kingdom* (Boston: Little Brown, 1941) for a friendship between a priest and an atheist physician; Doris Lessing, *The Diaries of Jane Somers* (New York:

.

Vintage Books, 1984) for a friendship between a working-class old woman and an elegant fashion editor/writer; Van Wyck Brooks, *Helen Keller* (New York: E. P. Dutton, 1956) for the friendship between the triply handicapped Keller and her teacher, Anne Sullivan; and Patrick O'Brian's Aubrey/Maturin series (17 books, New York: W. W. Norton) for a friendship between a rugged naval officer and a pacifist physician/botanist.

CHAPTER THIRTEEN

Looking Back, Looking Ahead

THE MODEL OF MORAL EDUCATION developed through care ethics is process oriented. It involves modeling, dialogue, practice, and confirmation. In this process orientation, it resembles Dewey's pragmatic naturalism and, more generally, the liberal tradition. There is an openness to great variety in what we model, talk about, practice, and approve in confirmation.

However, there is also content in the care model. There is an anchor to hold us steady. We learn as carers to respond as positively to others as the situation, our capacities, and values allow. The principle of caring is not a prescriptive principle in the traditional sense and has little persuasive force for anyone not already trained and dedicated to caring as a way of life. It is a principle in the descriptive sense: it describes how carers behave. In its emphasis on training (or better, education) and practice, it acknowledges a strong similarity to character education.

But what grounds the commitment to care, to respond positively, and what puts limits on that response? An ethic of care—at least as I have described it—is grounded in the human condition. Every human being requires care initially in order to survive, and that need—changing in form over time—continues as the organism grows. A healthy teenager does not need the sort of care required by an infant, and a mature adult does not require the care he or she once needed as a teenager. But every human being, at every stage of life, hopes for some form of positive response from other human beings. No one wants to be harmed by others or to live in fear of them. Everyone hopes for a helping hand in time of danger or more trouble than he or she can handle alone. Everyone wants enough respect to maintain at least minimal dignity.

Is this description of the universal desire to be cared for sufficient to ground an ethic? It would not be sufficient if we insisted on moving from a description of what *is* to a prescription of what *should be* by means of strict syllogistic logic. But human reasoning and rationality run broader and deeper than syllogistic reasoning. It is entirely reasonable to say that the caring response is fundamental in moral life because the desire to be cared for is universal. Indeed, some psychologists and anthropologists claim that the caring response is itself built-in and "natural" (Wilson, 1993). However, if it is, it carries with it a vulnerability to erosion that is not found in the desire to be cared for. The worse things get, the more desperately we want to be cared for; but, as troubles and pains bear directly on us, as our peers become cruel, as conditions in general worsen, many of us become less likely to care. We have to ask, then, how the caring response is developed and maintained.

If the value of the caring response depends on a universal desire for care (in the form of a positive response), why can't we formulate the care principle along the lines of the Golden Rule, Do unto others as you would have them do unto you? First, this commandment (or any commandment) means little to those who have not already learned to act by it; it has little persuasive force in itself. This, I think is a great insight of the character education tradition. But second, the usual wording of the Golden Rule is troubling to care theorists. Does it mean that we should treat others exactly as we ourselves would want to be treated? Care theorists will probably agree at the level of some form of positive response, but many of us will shrink from universalizing the particular response. We want to avoid the well-intentioned arrogance of the liberal tradition; that is, we believe that people want different outcomes, treasure different values, and express different needs. In a given situation, you may want a response that is very different from the one I would desire. Recognizing the inevitable otherness of each person (Derrida, 1978; Levinas, 1989; Lingis, 1994), we put great emphasis on receptive attention, or engrossment. To create a satisfactory response, I cannot simply consult my own preferences; I must find out what need the other is seeking to satisfy. In preparing to respond to you, I assume neither that your needs (beyond basic biological needs) are exactly like mine nor that people "like you" cannot possibly have needs like mine. I remain open and attentive to what you will disclose.

Now, how is this response delimited? It is obvious that every response is limited by contingent conditions. I cannot contribute a million dollars that I do not have. I cannot myself relieve a pain that requires expert medical attention. And so on. But, if satisfying an expressed need is within my capacities, should I always do so? Clearly, a yes answer to this would open the door to both nonsense and horrors. If you want to eliminate your neighbors and seek my help, I am not going to give it. Why not? Particular caring responses are always formulated within a framework of the relevant web, or network, of care. I must (this is an internal "I must," not an external principle) respond with care to your neighbor, too, and so I will not help you to eliminate him. However, I am dedicated to responding to you in such a way that you will understand, and in the best case, accept my response. I will try to maintain a caring relation even if I despise what you are trying to do because, in the long run, that relation should work for the best relations throughout the web of care.

It is worth emphasizing at this point that care theory recognizes the contribution of the cared-for to both the relation and to moral life more generally. A cared-for who is cruel and vicious to others—even if he or she is loving or accepting toward a particular carer—makes it very difficult to maintain a caring relation. One's capacity to care may be weakened or strengthened by how particular cared-fors treat others (Oliner & Oliner, 1988; Schulman, in press). Children make it easier or harder to parent them and their siblings; students make it easier or harder to teach well; patients make it easier or harder for physicians to treat them effectively. It is this philosophically unrecognized but enormously important contribution of the cared-for that leads care theorists to advocate cultivation of a variety of virtues beyond the narrowly moral. Contrary to Kant, we do bear some responsibility (a lot!) for the moral perfection of others.

Another advantage of emphasizing the relational sense of caring is that much of the mystery of altruism is removed. Because we human beings are defined in relation and because caring relations (and encounters) are so important to us, the acts we "do for others" are not entirely for others. If these acts strengthen the relations in which we are defined, they promote our well-being, too. In individualistic thought, such acts might be labeled "egoistic" because they benefit the self, but in relational ethics, neither "egoistic" nor "altruistic" is an accurate label for many generous and helpful acts. Of course, there remain some acts of complete self-sacrifice that benefit the doer only in relational memory, and there are acts performed purely for the actor's sake that incidentally benefit others. The terms "egoistic" and "altruistic" cannot be entirely eliminated from moral language, but they refer to a much smaller domain of acts.

As we look back at what has been thought and practiced in moral education and begin to look ahead, we can see some promising signs in recent work. For example, there is a trend toward the Deweyan definition of moral education; that is, more thinkers are emphasizing the moral conduct of education (Goodlad, Soder, & Sirotnik, 1993; Goodman & Lesnick, 2001; Hansen, 1993, 1995; Hostetler, 1997; Noddings, 1992; Sizer & Sizer, 1999; Sockett, 1993; Strike & Ternasky, 1993; Tom, 1984). This trend should support a wave of reflection, and perhaps resistance to the present overemphasis on testing and standardization.

Another good sign is that many practical books and programs are being introduced to help teachers in the work of moral education. (See, in addition to those mentioned in earlier chapters, Charney, 1992; Ryan & Bohlin,

1998; and the guides produced by the Developmental Studies Center, the Character Education Partnership, the Northeast Foundation for Children, and Teaching from Our Hearts.) These works should be critically and appreciatively reviewed by those interested in theory. We can learn from one another.

The potential for learning from one another should be underscored. There is now at least some agreement among psychologists, philosophers, and educators on the importance of certain key concepts. Martin Hoffman (2000), for example, uses a definition of empathy that closely resembles my "engrossment." He treats empathy as a "vicarious affective response to another person" (p. 29), rejecting the more usual Western definition that emphasizes cognitive understanding of another's state of mind (for a helpful history of the concept, see Verducci, 2000). In care theory, engrossment, or nonselective attention, receives what is there in another, and motivational displacement impels us to act—to help, to share, to respond in some positive fashion. Hoffman also offers impressive evidence that the sort of direct intervention I described in Chapter 1 is very powerful. He calls such acts "inductions," but they clearly match the sequence I described earlier: pointing out to the child the effects of his act, insisting that such acts are unacceptable, and showing a better way. Conscientious parents and teachers have used this method for centuries. Today's thinking, however, tries to avoid punishment, shame, and negative deserts (J. Gilligan, 1992; Noddings, 2001, 2002).

Although there are encouraging signs of some confluence of thought, there are also deeply troubling signs. Hoffman, for example, does not even mention the current character education movement, and he ignores entirely much of the powerful moral thought contributed by feminists such as Brabeck (2000), Carol Gilligan (1982), Held (1993), and Ruddick (1989). Educators are often unaware of what philosophers are writing, philosophers ignore educators and psychologists, and even within disciplines scholars inexplicably ignore the work of colleagues that others see as indispensable. I should also mention the lack of interaction between religious and secular thought. Again, there is some movement in this direction (Sears & Carper, 1998; Noddings, 2001), but not nearly enough, and the end result is too often greater separation rather than cooperation. Admittedly, it is difficult to keep up with what is going on in so many different fields, but we could do better. Indeed, if we are to have a real effect on the world of practice, we *must* do better.

Character educators might agree with care theorists on expanding the range of qualities (or virtues) we seek to develop. If we start to talk seriously about the connection between character and personality, we might make progress in both theory and practice. In their study of non-Jewish rescuers of Jews during the Holocaust, Oliner and Oliner (1988) refer to an altruistic *personality*, not to character (see also Schulman, in press). This may be important. If by personality, we mean a relatively enduring set of internal predispositions, it becomes important to ask how such dispositions are formed, which ones we value, and how a deficit in one can be compensated for with another. We are reminded, too, that some people of otherwise upstanding character have done horrible things to their fellow human beings. People who are truthful, loyal to their country, obedient to authority, dutiful, and in some ways responsible can nevertheless commit crimes against humanity. If Alice Miller (1983) is right, it is possible to inculcate a set of virtues that nonetheless leave the person with dreadful flaws. Are these flaws of character or personality, and how do the characteristics of one affect the other? If they are flaws of character, does that mean that one virtue is more important than all others and that its absence can destroy good character? Does it mean that good "character" comprises a complete set of identifiable virtues and that the absence of any one vitiates the goodness of character? Can one have a good character and yet demonstrably lack one or two (or more) virtues? How often can one slip up on the exercise of a particular virtue and still be credited with "having" it?

This last question reminds us of John Dewey's wisdom in rejecting the notion that virtue and intelligence are possessions. Both must be assessed in connection with action, and it may be less problematic to speak of a virtuous act than of a virtuous person. This is another reason for deemphasizing the virtue sense of caring. We can acknowledge that X intended to care for Y when she performed act A, but to assess the relation, we need to know how Y responded and whether the status of relation (X, Y) merits the label "caring."

In a similar vein, I think we make a mistake if we concentrate entirely on *inculcating* certain traits or virtues. The idea of inculcating virtues suggests, again, that they can become possessions. We need much more emphasis on understanding. Here we might work cooperatively with Kohlbergians and even with the more Deweyan advocates of values clarification (see Kirschenbaum, 1992; Leming, 1997). But the effort to encourage understanding should not be limited to reasoning about justice. Teenagers need to study accounts of people gone wrong. How does it happen that some people become vicious criminals? How does it happen that "good" citizens ignore the misery around them? How does patriotism sometimes become warped into cruelty? What makes it possible for one person to torture another? Novels, biographies, poetry, films, and historical accounts are all useful here, but they cannot be chosen just for inspiration. We need what Jung called "a morality of evil" to understand our own propensities toward evil.

Such study could help in another way. Many young people today are influenced by the current passion for "identity politics." There has always been a temptation for people to glorify their own nation, religion, and race. When that temptation is rejected, the alternative is often cynicism. Moral education that concentrates on empathy/attention and self-understanding should help students come to both healthy appreciation of their own groups and traditions and intelligent criticism of those same groups and traditions. It should not be necessary to turn our backs entirely on our own nation (religion, race) in order to recognize its faults. Neither is it necessary to insist, "Our country right or wrong," in order to be good citizens.

Closely connected to the critical/appreciative study of collective characteristics and traditions is the study of political partisanship. Political rhetoric today is so filled with self-righteousness and hypocrisy that it is difficult to introduce students to politics with any honest enthusiasm. Strictly speaking, the reform of political language is not a problem of moral education for the schools, but students surely need help in understanding how their feelings and subsequent reasoning are manipulated by partisan allegiance. Consider how, in the presidential election of 2000, formally powerful (closely reasoned) arguments have been diametrically opposed along party lines. Surely events such as these are strong evidence against the notion that people are moved by the force of better arguments. On the contrary, people (even those in supposedly nonpartisan positions of power) formulate arguments to support how they feel. The first step in educating against this way of operating (if we wish to change it), is to help people understand how feeling motivates both thought and action.

Perhaps people just are not moved by arguments at all. I am not alone in finding this possibility deplorable. We might be able to increase the possibility that people will be moved by good arguments through a deeper understanding of their own feelings. This suggests that schools should give far more attention to the education of affect than they do at present. Throughout this book, I have pointed to the importance of cultivating the moral sentiments and of helping students to understand what they are feeling. Not only is such education livelier and more likely to maintain students' attention, but it is also the key to moral motivation. To act morally, we have to be moved; we have to feel something.

Teacher educators should play a role in preparing teachers to handle affective education sensitively and effectively. Preservice teachers should be helped to develop a catalog of stories and other accounts revealing clashes of feelings and a wide range of affectively powerful material from history, biography, and the arts. It is not sufficient to provide teachers with a set of activities designed just for moral education and leave them with nothing morally relevant to use in their subject matter classes. This makes it as easy to ignore morality as it is for most people to ignore mathematics.

Finally, those charged with the task of moral education must keep in mind both senses of that expression. In agreement with character educators, care theorists want to produce good people. But we believe that the best way to do this is to concentrate on the conditions of educating—to provide an education that is morally defensible. Children who are genuinely and continuously cared for usually turn out to be reasonably good people. Thus when things go wrong or threaten to do so, we have to reflect on our own actions and beliefs. It is not just a matter of tightening up the rules, getting tougher, being consistent about penalties, teaching "them" what's right. It is more a matter of bringing relations into caring equilibrium, balancing expressed and inferred needs, and helping children understand both our actions and their own. There are no guarantees in moral education just as there are none in, say, mathematics education. But happy, well-cared for people do not usually commit acts of violence, deceit, or neglect. To produce good people we must provide a morally good education.

References

Abbott, E. A. (1952). *Flatland*. New York: Dover Books.

Aristotle (1985). *Nicomachean ethics* (T. Irwin, Trans.). Indianapolis: Hackett.

Augustine (1964). *On free choice of the will* (A. Benjamin & L. H. Hackstaff, Trans.). New York: Macmillan.

Baer, R. A., & Carper, J. C. (1998–1999). Spirituality and the public schools: An evangelical perspective. *Educational Leadership, 56*(4), 33–37.

Barrett, W. (1962). *Irrational man: A study in existential philosophy*. Garden City: Anchor Books.

Bates, S. (1995). A textbook of virtues. *New York Times*, Jan. 8, Education Life section.

Baumrind, D. (1993). Sex differences in moral reasoning: Response to Walker's (1984) conclusion that there are none. In M. J. Larrabee (Ed.), *An ethic of care* (pp. 177–192). New York: Routledge.

Beauvoir, S. de. (1952). *The second sex* (H. M. Parshley, Trans.). New York: Bantam Books.

Becher, J. (Ed.). (1990). *Women, religion and sexuality*. Philadelphia: Trinity Press.

Belenky, M. F., Clinchy, B. M., Goldberger, N. R., & Tarule, J. M. (1986). *Women's ways of knowing*. New York: Basic Books.

Bell, E. T. (1965). *Men of mathematics*. New York: Simon and Schuster. (Original work published 1937)

Bellah, R. N., Madsen, R., Sullivan, W. M., Swidler, A., & Tipton, S. M. (1985). *Habits of the heart*. Berkeley: University of California Press.

Benhabib, S. (1987). The generalized and the concrete other. In S. Benhabib & D. Cornell (Eds.), *Feminism as critique* (pp. 77–95). Minneapolis: University of Minnesota Press.

Bennett, W. J. (1993). *The book of virtues: A treasury of great moral stories*. New York: Simon and Schuster.

Berlin, I. (1969). Two concepts of liberty. In I. Berlin, *Four essays on liberty* (pp. 118–172). Oxford: Oxford University Press.

Bernard, J. (1975). *The future of motherhood*. New York: Penguin.

Bernstein, R. J. (1992). *The new constellation*. Cambridge: MIT Press.

Bettelheim, B. (1976). *The uses of enchantment: The meaning and importance of fairy tales*. New York: Knopf.

Black, N. (1983). Virginia Woolf: The life of natural happiness. In D. Spender (Ed.), *Feminist theorists* (pp. 296–313). New York: Pantheon.

Blount, J. M. (1998). *Destined to rule the schools.* Albany: State University of New York Press.

Bok, S. (1979). *Lying: Moral choice in public and private life.* New York: Vintage Books.

Booth, W. C. (1988). *The vocation of a teacher.* Chicago: University of Chicago Press.

Brabeck, M. M. (Ed.). (2000). *Practicing feminist ethics in psychology.* Washington, DC: American Psychological Association.

Buber, M. (1958). *Paths in utopia.* Boston: Beacon Press. (Original work published 1949)

Buber, M. (1965). *Between man and man.* New York: Macmillan.

Buber, M. (1970). *I and Thou* (W. Kaufmann, Trans.). New York: Scribner's. (Original work published 1958)

Buck, P. (1936). *The exile.* New York: Triangle.

Buck, P. (1936). *Fighting angel.* New York: John Day.

Burbules, N. (1993). *Dialogue in teaching.* New York: Teachers College Press.

Burnyeat, M. F. (1980). Aristotle on learning to be good. In A. M. Rorty (Ed.), *Essays on Aristotle's ethics* (pp. 69–92). Berkeley: University of California Press.

Cahn, S. M. (Ed.). (1997). *Classic and contemporary readings in the philosophy of education.* New York: McGraw-Hill.

Carter, R. E. (1984). *Dimensions of moral education.* Toronto: University of Toronto Press.

Casey, E. S. (1993). *Getting back into place.* Bloomington: Indiana University Press.

Charney, R. (1992). *Teaching children to care.* Greenfield, MN: Northeast Foundation for Children.

Chazan, B. (1985). *Contemporary approaches to moral education.* New York: Teachers College Press.

Chodorow, N. (1978). *The reproduction of mothering.* Berkeley: University of California Press.

Cohen, M. (1995). *Lewis Carroll.* New York: Knopf.

Coles, R. (1989). *The call of stories: Teaching and the moral imagination.* Boston: Houghton Mifflin.

Collins, P. H. (1990). *Black feminist thought.* Boston: Unwin Hyman.

Colsant, L. C. (1995). "Hey, man, why do we gotta take this?" Learning to listen to students. In J. G. Nicholls & T. A. Thorkildsen (Eds.), *Reasons for learning* (pp. 62–89). New York: Teachers College Press.

Comer, J. P. (1988). Is "parenting" essential to good teaching? *NEA Today, 6,* 34–40.

Crocco, M. S., & Davis, O. L. (Eds.). (1999). *Bending the future to their will.* Lanham, MD: Rowman and Littlefield.

Daly, M. (1974). *Beyond God the father.* Boston: Beacon Press.

Daly, M. (1984). *Pure lust.* Boston: Beacon Press.

Damon, W. (1988). *The moral child: Nurturing children's natural moral growth.* New York: Free Press.

Derrida, J. (1978). *Writing and difference* (Alan Bass, Trans.). Chicago: University of Chicago Press.

Dewey, J. (1916). *Democracy and education*. New York: Macmillan.

Dewey, J. (1930). *Human nature and conduct*. New York: Modern Library.

Dewey, J. (1963). *Experience and education*. New York: Macmillan. (Original work published 1938)

Dewey, J. (1972). Ethical principles underlying education. In J. A. Boydston (Ed.), *The early works, 1882–1898* (Vol. 5, pp. 54–83). Carbondale: Southern Illinois University Press. (Original work published 1897)

Dewey, J. (1990). *The school and society* and *The child and the curriculum*. Chicago: University of Chicago Press. (Original works published 1900 and 1902)

Dewey, J., & Tufts, J. (1978). *Ethics*. In J. A. Boydston (Ed.), *The middle works, 1899–1924* (Vol. 5). Carbondale: Southern Illinois Press. (Original work published 1908)

Dickens, C. (1853). *Bleak house* (Vol. 2). New York: Peter Fenelon.

Dinnerstein, D. (1976). *The mermaid and the minotaur: Sexual arrangements and human malaise*. New York: Harper.

Du Bois, W. E. B. (1989). *The souls of black folk*. New York: Bantam Books. (Original work published 1903)

Eisler, R. (1987). *The chalice and the blade*. New York: HarperCollins.

Erdrich, L. (1993). The veils. In E. Buchwald, P. Fletcher, & M. Roth (Eds.), *Transforming a rape culture* (pp. 335–339). Minneapolis: Milkweed Editions.

Erikson, E. (1969). *Gandhi's truth*. New York: W. W. Norton.

Etzioni, A. (1993). *The spirit of community*. New York: Touchstone.

Franz, M. L. von. (1983). *Shadow and evil in fairy tales*. Dallas, TX: Spring.

Fraser, N. (1996). *Social justice in the age of identity politics: Redistribution, recognition, and participation*. Tanner Lecture on Human Values, Stanford University.

Freire, P. (1970). *Pedagogy of the oppressed* (M. B. Ramos, Trans.). New York: Herder & Herder.

Fukuyama, F. (1995). *Trust: The social virtues and the creation of prosperity*. New York: Free Press.

Gardner, H. (1983). *Frames of mind*. New York: Basic Books.

Gardner, J. W. (1961). *Excellence: Can we be equal and excellent too?* New York: Harper.

Gardner, J. W. (1991). *Building community*. Washington, DC: Independent Sector.

Gardner, M. (1963). *The annotated Alice (Lewis Carroll)*. New York: World.

Garrod, A. (1993). *Approaches to moral development*. New York: Teachers College Press.

Gentile, G. (1960). *Genesis and structure of society* (H. S. Harris, Trans.). Urbana: University of Illinois Press.

Gilligan, C. J. (1982). *In a different voice*. Cambridge: Harvard University Press.

Gilligan, J. (1992). *Violence*. New York: Putnam's Sons.

Glendon, M. A. (1991). *Rights talk*. New York: Free Press.

Goodlad, J., Soder, R., & Sirotnik, K. (Eds.). (1993). *The moral dimensions of teaching*. San Francisco: Jossey-Bass.

Goodman, J. F., & Lesnick, H. (2001). *The moral stake in education*. New York: Longman.

Gordon, M. (1980). *The company of women.* New York: Ballantine Books.

Gordon, S., Benner, P., & Noddings, N. (Eds.). (1996). *Caregiving.* Philadelphia: University of Pennsylvania Press.

Gouinlock, J. (Ed.). (1994). *The moral writings of John Dewey.* Amherst, NY: Prometheus Books.

Graham, J. (1999). *It's up to us.* Langley, WA: The Giraffe Project.

Green, T. (1968). A topology of the teaching concept. In C. J. B. Macmillan & T. Nelson (Eds.), *Concepts of Teaching* (pp. 28–62). Chicago: Rand McNally.

Green, T. (1988). The economy of virtue. *American Journal of Education, 96,* 127–142.

Grumet, M. R. (1988). *Bitter Milk.* Amherst: University of Massachusetts Press.

Habermas, J. (1990). *Moral consciousness and communicative action* (C. Lenhardt & S. W. Nicholsen, Trans.). Cambridge: MIT Press. (Original work published 1983)

Hansen, D. (1993). From role to person: The moral layeredness of classroom teaching. *American Educational Research Journal, 30,* 651–674.

Hansen, D. (1995). *The call to teach.* New York: Teachers College Press.

Harding, M. E. (1976). *Woman's mysteries.* New York: Harper Colophon Books.

Hartshorne, H., & May, M. (1928–1930). *Studies in the nature of character* (Vols. 1–3). New York: Macmillan.

Haught, J. A. (1990). *Holy horrors.* Buffalo: Prometheus Press.

Hawkins, D. (1973). How to plan for spontaneity. In C. E Silberman (Ed.), *The open classroom reader* (pp. 486–503). New York: Vintage Books.

Heartwood Institute. (n.d.). *Heartwood Curriculum.* Pittsburgh: Author.

Hechinger, F. (1994). Saving youth from violence. *Carnegie Quarterly, 39*(1), 2–15.

Held, V. (1993). *Feminist morality.* Chicago: University of Chicago Press.

Heslep, R. D. (1995). *Moral education for Americans.* Westport, CT: Praeger.

Hitler, A. (1939). *Mein Kampf.* New York: Reynal & Hitchcock. (Original work published 1925)

Hoffman, M. L. (2000). *Empathy and moral development.* Cambridge: Cambridge University Press.

Hostetler, K. D. (1997). *Ethical judgment in teaching.* Boston: Allyn & Bacon.

hooks, b. (1993). Seduced by violence no more. In E. Buchwald, P. Fletcher, & M. Roth (Eds.), *Transforming a rape culture* (pp. 353–357). Minneapolis: Milkweed Editions.

Hume, D. (1983). *An enquiry concerning the principles of morals.* Indianapolis: Hackett. (Original work published 1751)

Institute for Education in Transformation. (1992). *Voices from the inside.* Claremont, CA: Claremont Graduate School.

Jackson, P. W. (1992). *Untaught lessons.* New York: Teachers College Press.

Jackson, P. W., Boostrom, R. E., & Hansen, D. (1993). *The moral life of schools.* San Francisco: Jossey-Bass.

James, W. (1929). *The varieties of religious experience.* New York: Modern Library. (Original work published 1902).

Jung, C. G. (1969). *Collected works* (Vol. 2). Reprints. Princeton: Princeton University Press.

Katz, M., Noddings, N., & Strike, K. (Eds.). (1999). *Justice and caring*. New York: Teachers College Press.

Kerber, L. (1997). *Toward an intellectual history of women*. Chapel Hill: University of North Carolina Press.

Kimmel, M. S. (1993). Clarence, William, Iron Mike, tailhook, Senator Packwood, spur posse, magic . . . and us. In E. Buchwald, P. Fletcher, & M. Roth (Eds.), *Transforming a rape culture* (pp. 121–138). Minneapolis: Milkweed Editions.

Kirschenbaum, H. (1992, June). A comprehensive model for values education and moral education. *Phi Delta Kappan*, pp. 771–776.

Knowles, J. (1959). *A separate peace*. New York: Macmillan.

Kohlberg, L. (1981). *The philosophy of moral development* (Vol. 1). San Francisco: Harper & Row.

Kohn, A. (1993). *Punished by rewards: The trouble with gold stars, incentive plans, A's, praise, and other bribes*. Boston: Houghton Mifflin.

Kozol, J. (1991). *Savage inequalities*. New York: Crown.

Kushner, H. (1981). *When bad things happen to good people*. New York: Schocken Books.

Leacock, S. (1956). Common sense and the universe. In J. R. Newman (Ed.), *The world of mathematics* (Vol 4, pp. 2460–2469). New York: Simon and Schuster.

Leming, J. (1993). *Character education: Lessons from the past, models for the future*. Camden, ME: Institute for Global Ethics.

Leming, J. (1997). Research and practice in character education: A historical perspective. In A. Molnar (Ed.), *The construction of children's character* (pp. 31–44). Chicago: National Society for the Study of Education.

Levinas, E. (1989). *The Levinas reader* (S. Hand, Ed.). Oxford: Blackwell.

Lewis, C. S. (1955). *The abolition of man: How education develops man's sense of morality*. New York: Collier Books.

Lickona, T. (1991). *Educating for character: How our schools can teach respect and responsibility*. New York: Bantam Books.

Lickona, T., Schaps, E., & Lewis, C. (1998). *Eleven principles of effective character education*. Washington, DC: Character Education Partnership.

Lingis, A. (1994). *The community of those who have nothing in common*. Bloomington: Indiana University Press.

Lipman, M. (1991). *Thinking in education*. Cambridge: Cambridge University Press.

Lyons, N. P. (1983). Two perspectives: On self, relationships, and morality. *Harvard Educational Review, 53*(2), 125–145.

MacIntyre, A. (1981). *After virtue*. Notre Dame: University of Notre Dame Press.

MacIntyre, A. (1988). *Whose justice? Which rationality?* Notre Dame: University of Notre Dame Press.

Maguire, D. C. (1982, March 15). The feminization of God and ethics. *Christianity and crisis*, pp. 59–67.

Martin, J. R. (1984). Bringing women into educational thought. *Educational Theory, 34*(4), 341–354.

Martin, J. R. (1985). *Reclaiming a conversation*. New Haven: Yale University Press.

Martin, J. R. (1992). *The schoolhome: Rethinking schools for changing families*. Cambridge: Harvard University Press.

Martin, J.R. (1995). A philosophy of education for the year 2000. *Phi Delta Kappan, 76*(5), 355–359.

Mayeaux, A. R. (1993). Towards the fifth centenary: Dominicans, the "other" and the unavowable community. *Providence, 1*(3), 259–271.

McCarthy, T. (1978). *The critical theory of Jürgen Habermas.* Cambridge: MIT Press.

McClellan, B. E. (1999). *Moral education in America.* New York: Teachers College Press.

McPeck, J. E. (1981). *Critical thinking in education.* Oxford: Martin Robertson.

Mehan, H. (1979). *Learning lessons.* Cambridge: Harvard University Press.

Mill, J. S. (1993). *On liberty* and *Utilitarianism.* New York: Bantam Books. (Original works published 1859 and 1871)

Miller, A. (1983). *For your own good* (H. Hannun & H. Hannun, Trans.). New York: Farrar, Straus, Giroux.

Molnar, A. (Ed.). (1997). *The construction of children's character.* Chicago: National Society for the Study of Education.

Nash, G. H. (1979). *The conservative movement in America.* New York: Basic Books.

Nash, R. J. (1997). *Answering the "virtuecrats."* New York: Teachers College Press.

Naylor, T. H., Willimon, W. H., & Naylor, M. R. (1994). *The search for meaning.* Nashville: Abingdon Press.

Neumann, E. (1955). *The great mother.* Princeton: Princeton University Press.

Newman, J. H., Cardinal. (1964). Liberal knowledge its own end. In L. A. Fiedler & J. Vinocur (Eds.), *The continuing debate* (pp. 31–50). New York: St. Martin's Press.

Nietzsche, F. (1973). *Beyond good and evil.* London: Penguin. (Original work published 1886)

Nisbet, R. A. (1953). *The quest for community.* New York: Oxford University Press.

Noble, D. F. (1992). *A world without women.* Oxford: Oxford University Press.

Noddings, N. (1984). *Caring: A feminine approach to ethics and moral education.* Berkeley: University of California Press.

Noddings, N. (1989). *Women and evil.* Berkeley: University of California Press.

Noddings, N. (1991). Stories in dialogue: Caring and interpersonal reasoning. In C. Witherell & N. Noddings (Eds.), *Stories lives tell: Narrative and dialogue in Education* (pp. 157–170). New York: Teachers College Press.

Noddings, N. (1992). *The challenge to care in schools.* New York: Teachers College Press.

Noddings, N. (1993). *Educating for intelligent belief or unbelief.* New York: Teachers College Press.

Noddings, N. (2000). Two concepts of caring. In R. Curren (Ed.), *Philosophy of Education 1999* (pp. 36–39). Urbana, IL: Philosophy of Education Society.

Noddings, N. (2001). Public schooling, democracy, and religious dissent. In J. Goodlad, R. Soder, & T. McMannon (Eds.), *Developing democratic character in the young.* San Francisco: Jossey-Bass.

Noddings, N. (2002). *Starting at home: Care and social policy.* Berkeley: University of California Press.

Norris, S. R. (1992). *The generalizability of critical thinking.* New York: Teachers College Press.

Nucci, L. P. (Ed.). (1989). *Moral development and character education*. Berkeley: McCutchan.

Nussbaum, M. (1986). *The fragility of goodness*. Cambridge: Cambridge University Press.

Oakeshott, M. (1984). Political education. In M. Sandel (Ed.), *Liberalism and its critics* (pp. 219–238). New York: New York University Press.

Oliner, S., & Oliner, P. M. (1988). *The altruistic personality: Rescuers of Jews in Nazi Europe*. New York: Free Press.

Orwell, G. (1949). *Nineteen eighty-four*. New York: Harcourt Brace Jovanovich.

Orwell, G. (1946/1981). *A collection of essays*. San Diego: Harcourt Brace.

Paul, R. (1990). *Critical thinking: What every person needs to survive in a rapidly changing world*. Rohnert Park, CA: Center for Critical Thinking and Moral Critique.

Perry, W. (1970). *Forms of intellectual and ethical development in the college years*. New York: Holt, Rinehart & Winston.

Peshkin, A. (1986). *God's choice: The total world of a fundamentalist Christian school*. Chicago: University of Chicago Press.

Phillips, J. A. (1984). *Eve: The history of an idea*. San Francisco: Harper & Row.

Piaget, J. (1965). *The moral judgment of the child*. New York: Free Press. (Original work published 1932)

Posner, M. (1994). Research raises troubling questions about violence prevention programs. *Harvard Education Letter, 10*(3), 1–4.

Power, F. C., Higgins, A., & Kohlberg, L. (1989). *Lawrence Kohlberg's approach to moral education*. New York: Columbia University Press.

Purpel, D. E. (1989). *The moral and spiritual crisis in education*. New York: Bergin and Garvey.

Quint, S. (1994). *Schooling homeless children*. New York: Teachers College Press.

Rawls, J. (1971). *A theory of justice*. Cambridge: Harvard University Press.

Reverby, S. (1987). *Ordered to care*. Cambridge: Cambridge University Press.

Rice, S. (1996). Dewey's conception of "virtue" and its implications for moral education. *Educational Theory, 46*(3), 269–282.

Ricoeur, P. (1969). *The symbolism of evil*. Boston: Beacon Press.

Rossiter, M. W. (1982). *Women scientists in America: Struggles and strategies to 1940*. Baltimore: Johns Hopkins University Press.

Ruddick, S. (1980). Maternal thinking. *Feminist Studies, 6*(2), 342–367.

Ruddick, S. (1984). Preservative love and military destruction: Some reflections on mothering and peace. In J. Trebilcot (Ed.), *Mothering: Essays in feminist theory* (pp. 231–262). Totowa, NJ: Rowman & Allenheld.

Ruddick, S. (1989). *Maternal thinking: Towards a politics of peace*. Boston: Beacon Press.

Ruether, R. R. (1983). *Sexism and God-talk*. Boston: Beacon Press.

Ryan, K., & Bohlin, K. E. (1998). *Building character in schools*. San Francisco: Jossey-Bass.

Rybczynski, W. (1986). *Home: A short history of an idea*. New York: Viking.

Salton, S. (1992, August 30). Pro-life + pro-choice = common ground. *San Francisco Chronicle*, pp. A 15.

Sanford, J. A. (1981). *Evil: The shadow side of reality*. New York: Crossroad.

Sarton, M. (1970). *Kinds of love.* New York: W. W. Norton.

Saunders, H. H. (1991). *The other walls.* Princeton: Princeton University Press.

Schlesinger, A. M., Jr. (1992). *The disuniting of America: Reflections on a multicultural society.* New York: W. W. Norton.

Schulman, M. (in press). How we become moral: The sources of moral motivation. In *Handbook of Positive Psychology.* Oxford: Oxford University Press.

Sears, J. T., & Carper, J. C. (Eds.). (1998). *Curriculum, religion, and public education.* New York: Teachers College Press.

Selznick, P. (1992). *The moral commonwealth.* Berkeley: University of California Press.

Sergiovanni, T. J. (1994). *Building community in schools.* San Francisco: Jossey-Bass.

Shange, N. (1993). Comin' to terms. In E. Buchwald, P. Fletcher, & M. Roth (Eds.), *Transforming a rape culture* (pp. 369–374). Minneapolis: Milkweed Editions.

Sichel, B. A. (1988). *Moral education: Character, community, and ideals.* Philadelphia: Temple University Press.

Siegel, H. (1988). *Educating reason: Rationality, critical thinking and education.* New York: Routledge.

Simon, K. G. (1997). *The place of meaning: A study of the moral, existential, and intellectual in American high schools.* Unpublished doctoral dissertation, Stanford University.

Sizer, T. R., & Sizer, N. F. (1999). *The students are watching: Schools and the moral contract.* Boston: Beacon Press.

Slote, M. (1992). *From morality to virtue.* New York: Oxford University Press.

Slote, M. (1998). Caring in the balance. In M. S. Halfon & J. G. Haber (Eds.), *Norms and values* (pp. 27–36). Lanham, MD: Rowman & Littlefield.

Slote, M. (2000). Caring versus the philosophers. In R. Curren (Ed.), *Philosophy of education 1999* (pp. 25–35). Urbana: University of Illinois and Philosophy of Education Society.

Sockett, H. (1993). *The moral base for teacher preparation.* New York: Teachers College Press.

Sommers, T., & Shields, L. (1987). *Women take care.* Gainesville, FL: Triad.

Stone, M. (1976). *When God was a woman.* New York: Dial Press.

Stowe, H. B. (1991). *Uncle Tom's cabin.* Pleasantville, NY: Reader's Digest. (Original work published 1852).

Strike, K. A., & Ternasky, P. L. (Eds.). (1993). *Ethics for professionals in education.* New York: Teachers College Press.

Tappan, M., & Packer, M. (Eds.). (1991). *Narrative and storytelling: Implications for understanding and moral development.* San Francisco: Jossey-Bass.

Taylor, C. (1989). *Sources of the self.* Cambridge: Harvard University Press.

Teaching from Our Hearts Network. Mkirs54321@aol.com

Thayer-Bacon, B. (2000). *Transforming critical thinking.* New York: Teachers College Press.

Thinking: The Journal of Philosophy for Children. Upper Montclair, NJ: Montclair State University.

Thompson, P. J. (1992). *Bringing feminism home.* Charlottetown, Canada: Home Economics Publishing Collective.

Tillich, P. (1952). *The courage to be*. New Haven: Yale University Press.

Tom, A. (1984). *Teaching as a moral craft*. New York: Longman.

Turner, F. (1991). *Rebirth of value: Meditations on beauty, ecology, religion, and education*. Albany: State University of New York Press.

Verducci, S. (2000). A conceptual history of empathy and a question it raises for moral education. *Educational Theory, 50*(1), 63–80.

Vitz, P. (1990). The use of stories in moral development. *American Psychologist, 45*(6), 709–720.

Waerness, K. (1996). The rationality of caring. In S. Gordon, P. Benner, & N. Noddings (Eds.), *Caregiving* (pp. 231–255). Philadelphia: University of Pennsylvania Press.

Walzer, M. (1990). A critique of philosophical conversation. In M. Kelly (Ed.), *Hermeneutics and critical theory in ethics and politics* (pp. 182–196). Cambridge: MIT Press.

Weaver, R. (1948). *Ideas have consequences*. Chicago: University of Chicago Press.

Weber, M. (1958). *The Protestant ethic and the spirit of capitalism* (T. Parsons, Trans.). New York: Scribner's. (Original work published 1904–1905)

Weil, S. (1977). *Simone Weil reader* (G. A. Panichas, Ed.). Reprints. Mount Kisco, NY: Moyer Bell Limited.

Weiler, K. (1998). *Country schoolwomen*. Stanford: Stanford University Press.

Welter, B. (1996). The cult of true womanhood: 1820–1860. *American Quarterly, 18*, 151–174.

White, J. T. (1909). *Character lessons in American biography*. New York: Character Development League.

Wiesel, E. (1960). *Night* (S. Rodway, Trans.). New York: Hill and Wang.

Wiesel, E. (1989, March 19). Interview: Are we afraid of peace? *Parade Magazine*, p. 8.

Wiesenthal, S. (1976). *The sunflower*. New York: Schocken Books.

Wilshire, B. (1990). *The moral collapse of the university*. Albany: State University of New York Press.

Wilson, J. Q. (1993). *The moral sense*. New York: Free Press.

Woolf, V. (1966). *Collected Essays* (Vol 2). Reprints. London: Hogarth Press.

Wyschogrod, E. (1990). *Saints and postmodernism: Revisioning moral philosophy*. Chicago: University of Chicago Press.

Zeldin, T. (1994). *An intimate history of humanity*. New York: HarperCollins.

Index

A

Adamic myth, 105, 115
Affect, 70, 71, 80
Aims of education, 93–101
Algebra, 30, 31
Alice in Wonderland (Carroll), 134–135
All Quiet on the Western Front (Remarque), 43
Altruism, 150
Angel in the house, 55
Argument, 120, 121, 122, 128, 135, 153
Aristotle, xiii, 4, 16, 22, 37, 40, 44, 61, 67, 83, 97, 98, 137, 140
Arts, 81, 125
Attention and attentive love, 40, 95, 153
  interpersonal, 19
Augustine, 105
Austen, Jane, 141

B

Baer, Richard, 7, 15
Barrett, William, 106
Bates, Stephen, 7, 45, 69
Baumrind, Diana, 119, 120
Beauvoir, Simone de, 115
Becher, Jeanne, 52
Beecher, Catherine, 54

Belenky, Mary, 22
Bellah, Robert, et al., 64, 67
Benhabib, Seyla, 120
Bennett, William, 3
Berlin, Isaiah, 68
Bernard, Jessie, 102
Bernstein, Richard, 64, 121, 136
Bettelheim, Bruno, 62
Black culture, 35
Black, Naomi, 102
Bleak House (Dickens), 138–139
Blount, Jackie, 52
Bohlin, K. E., 150
Bok, Sissela, 23
Booth, Wayne, 124
Brabeck, Mary, 151
Buber, Martin, 20, 44
Burbules, Nicholas, 122

C

Cahn, Steven, 3
Care and Caring
  analysis of, 8–10
  caring for/caring about, 86
  and competence, 101
  and components of moral education, 15, 148
  and critical thinking, 39–58
  desire for, 21
  ethics and theory of, 1, 2, 8–10, 13–24, 91, 148, 149

Care and Caring (*continued*)
  learning to care, 25–38
  modeling of, 16
  practice in, 20
  relations of, 14, 15, 28, 85–89, 109,
      142, 150, 151, 152, 154
  themes of, 33–38, 44, 97, 100
  tradition of, 38, 51–58
  as virtue, 14, 27, 85–89
Cared-for, 28, 88
Caregiving, 56–58
Caring (Noddings), 85
Carnegie Quarterly, 25, 26
Carper, James, 7, 45, 151
Carroll, Lewis, 135
Carter, Robert, 122
Casey, Edward, 55
Character Development League, 23, 62
Character education, xiii, 1–8, 61–72,
      91, 123, 148, 152, 154
  and religion, 45, 48
Character Education Partnership
      (CEP), 3, 5, 151
Charney, Ruth, 150
Chazan, Barry, xiv
Chesterton, G.K., 135
Chodorow, Nancy, 102
Christianity, 104, 105, 115, 122
Classism, 71
Coercion, 28–32, 79, 100
Coles, Robert, 62, 124
Collins, Patricia, 121
Colsant, Lee, 143–144
Comer, James, 25
Common Ground, 17–18
Community, 10, 61–72
  dark side of, 66–67
  of memory, 64
  service, 20
Company of Women, The (Gordon),
      141
Competence theories, 120
Competition, 20
Confirmation, 20–21
Conservatism, 62–67

Consistency, 7
Continuity, 26–28
Conversation, 118–130, 131–147
  formal, 118–122, 132, 133–136
  immortal, 122–126, 132, 136–141
  moral criteria of, 129
  ordinary, 126–130, 142–146
Coverture, 56
Creation, 126, 137
Critical thinking, 39–58, 116
Crocco, Margaret, 52
"Crossgates," 79
Cultural literacy, 134–135
Curriculum topics, 36–38, 91, 94, 96,
      97, 112, 116, 137
  friendship, 36–38
  hierarchies of, 100
  homemaking, 53–55
  love, 36

D

Daly, Mary, 102, 105, 106
Damon, William, 5, 6
Darwin, Charles, 137
Democracy, 75
Derrida, Jacques, 67, 136, 149
Descartes, Rene, 33, 63, 125
Developmental Studies Center, 151
Dewey, John, 21, 22, 31, 73–84, 91,
      97, 128, 152
Dialogue, 16–19, 120
Dickens, Charles, 81, 86, 138
Dinnerstein, Dorothy, 102
Discourse ethics, 118–120
Dramatic rehearsal, 83
Du Bois, W.E.B., 139

E

Eisler, Riane, 52
Erdrich, Louise, 35
Erikson, Erik, 104

Ethical naturalism, 84
"Ethical Principles Underlying
    Education" (Dewey), 73–84
Ethics (Dewey & Tufts), 81, 83, 84
Etzioni, Amitai, 68
Evil, 34, 78, 102–106
    control of, 114–117
    morality of, 109, 116, 152
    projection of, 105, 115, 116
Exile, The (Buck), 113
Existential questions, 124, 136, 142

F

Fascism, 66–67
Feeling, 42, 45. *See also* Affect
Feminist perspectives, 102–117
    Black, 121
Fighting Angel (Buck), 113
Flatland (Abbott), 71–72
Force (energy, will), 79
Franz, Marie von, 106
Fraser, Nancy, 57
Frederick, Christine, 54
Freire, Paulo, 16
Friendship, 97, 140
Fukuyama, Francis, 66

G

Gandhi, 104
Gardner, Howard, 96
Gardner, John, 68, 96
Gardner, Martin, 134
Garrod, Andrew, 124
Gender stereotypes, 103
Gentile, Giovanni, 66
Gibbs, James, 88
Gilbreth, Lillian, 54
Gilligan, Carol, 22, 44, 108, 109, 151
Gilligan, James, 4
Giraffes (Heroes Program), 3
Glendon, Mary Ann, 66

God, 7, 33, 34, 40, 45, 69, 104, 105,
    106, 113, 116, 125
Golden rule, 149
Goodlad, John (and Soder &
    Sirotnik), 150
Good life, 137
Goodman, Joan, 150
Gordon, Mary, 141
Growth, 82, 112
Grumet, Madeleine, 110

H

Habermas, Jürgen, 118–122, 136
Habit, 82
Hamlet (Shakespeare), 104
Hansen, David, 133, 150
Harding, Esther, 103, 107, 115
Hartshorne, Hugh, xiii, 3
Hartshorne, May, xiii
Haught, James, 65–66
Hawkins, David, 145
Heartwood, 3, 45, 69
Held, Virginia, 151
Heslep, Robert, x
Hitler, Adolf, 66
Hoffman, Martin, 151
Holocaust, 43, 47–50, 152
hooks, bell, 35
Hostetler, Karl, 150
Hume, David, 2, 8, 41
Huxley, T. H., 137

I

Identity politics, 153
Indoctrination, 4, 42, 45

J

Jackson, Philip, 7, 70, 144
James, William, 108, 109, 125, 126

Julius Caesar (Shakespeare), 41
Jung, Carl, 103, 106, 108, 109, 115,
     116, 152

                    K

Karl (in *Sunflower*), 47–50
Katz, Michael, 19
Kant, Immanuel, 1, 14, 15, 23, 63, 81,
     118, 120, 150
Kerber, Linda, 52, 56, 58
Killing, 86–87, 98
Kimmel, Michael, 34
Kirschenbaum, Howard, 152
Knowles, John, 37
Kohlberg, Lawrence, xiii, xiv, 2, 3,
     22, 63, 119, 152
Kohn, Alfie, 7
Kozol, Jonathan, 33
Kushner, Harold, 34

                    L

Leacock, Stephen, 137
Leming, James, 152
Lesnick, H., 150
Levinas, Emmanuel, 10, 44, 149
Lewis, C.S., 42, 70, 71, 81
Liberal arts, 72, 94, 95, 123, 124
Liberalism, 64, 65, 66
   communitarian, 68, 69
Lickona, Thomas, 3, 5, 6, 7, 123
Lingis, Alfonso, 10, 149
Lipman, Matthew, 70
Logic, 133–136
Lyons, Nona, 44

                    M

MacArthur, Douglas, 117
MacIntyre, Alasdair, 1, 61, 62, 64, 67
Maguire, Daniel, 107, 114, 115
Manhood, 34–35, 109–114

Martin, Jane Roland, 38, 39, 52, 95,
     110–112, 114
Mathematics and moral education,
     71–72, 95, 125, 133–136, 140,
     142
Mayeaux, Ann Russell, 67
McCarthy, Thomas, 118
McClellan, B. Edward, 63
McGuffey readers, 63
McPeck, John, 39
Meno (Plato), 3
Mill, John Stuart, 73
Miller, Alice, 28–29, 123, 152
Molnar, Alex, xiv
Moral (ethical) conduct of education,
     73–77, 96, 99, 154
Moral dilemmas, 2
Moral imagination, 49
Moral judgment, 63, 79, 82, 119. *See
     also* Reason; Argument
Moral sensibility, 8, 41, 45, 46, 80,
     137. *See also* Feeling; Affect
Motherhood, 113
Motivation, 7, 8
Mysticism, 71, 125

                    N

Nash, George, 66
Nash, Robert, 3
Naylor, Thomas, 72
Nazism, 43, 47–50, 66, 69
Needs, 149
Newman, John Henry Cardinal, 123
Nicomachean Ethics (Aristotle), 61, 97
Nietzsche, Friedrich, 104, 105, 106, 115
Nineteen Eighty-Four (Orwell), 9
Nisbet, Robert, 64, 66
Noble, David, 52
Noddings, Nel, 2, 7, 13, 34, 44, 126
Norris, Stephen, 39
Northeast Foundation for Children,
     151
Nucci, Larry, xiv, 13
Nussbaum, Martha, 129

O

Oakeshott, Michael, 62, 64
Obligation, 13
Oliner, P., 8, 150, 152
Oliner, Samuel, 8, 150, 152
Orwell, George, 8, 79
Owen, Wilfred, 43, 70

P

Packer, M., 124
Pascal, Blaise, 33, 125
Pattison, Mary, 54
Paul, Richard, 46
Permissiveness, 79
Personality, 6
Perry, William, x
Peshkin, Alan, 122
Phillips, J. Anthony, 115
Piaget, Jean, xiv
Planning for teaching, 145
Plato, 3, 40, 52, 111, 125
Poisonous pedagogy, 29, 30
Political traditions, 62, 64
Posner, M., 27
Poverty, 94
Pragmatic naturalism, 13, 21
Pride and Prejudice (Austen), 141, 142
Protagoras (Plato), 3
Purpel, David, 70
Pythagoreans, 125

Q

Quint, Sharon, 27

R

Rawls, John, 65, 120
Reasoning, 118, 148. *See also* Argument; Moral judgment

Relativism, 6
Religion, 45, 48, 104–109, 112, 114–116, 122, 123
Remarque, Erich Maria, 71
Reverby, Susan, 52, 53
Rewards, 7
Rice, Suzanne, 82
Richards, Ellen, 54
Ricoeur, Paul, 104, 106
Rossiter, Margaret, 52
Ruddick, Sara, 26, 55, 98, 102, 108, 151
Ruether, Rosemary Radford, 106
Ryan, Kevin, 150
Rybczynski, Witold, 54

S

Sarton, May, 32
Saunders, Harold, 128
Schlesinger, Arthur, 63
Schulman, Michael, 150, 152
Science, 126, 137
Scopes trial, 137
Sears, James, 151
Selznick, Phillip, 67, 68
Separate Peace, A (Knowles), 37, 140
Sergiovanni, Thomas, 70
Sexism, 71
Shange, Ntozake, 35
Shields, L., 53
Sichel, Betty, 3, 61
Siegel, Harvey, 39, 46
Simon, Kathy, 34
Sizer, N., 150
Sizer, Theodore, 150
Slote, Michael, 2, 5, 6, 59, 85, 88
Social life, 75–77
    changes in, 93
    criteria for moral, 75–77, 82
    and intelligence, 75
Social studies, 51–58, 116
Sockett, Hugh, 150
Socrates, 3, 4, 40, 111, 120
Sommers, Tish, 53

Stone, Merlin, 115
Stories in moral education, 9, 33–38,
        42, 44–50, 70, 72, 81, 121, 123,
        125, 126, 131–147
    philosophical fictions as, 135
Stowe, Harriet Beecher, 38, 45, 46
Strike, Kenneth, 150
Sunflower, The (Wiesenthal), 47–50
Sylvester, James, 140

T

Tappan, Mark, 124
Taylor, Charles, 62
Teacher education, 153–154
Teachers as models, 144
Teaching from Our Hearts (Buildcare),
        151
Ternasky, P. L.
Thayer-Bacon, Barbara, 1, 44
Thompson, Patricia, 111
Tillich, Paul, 66, 67
Tom, Alan, 150
Torberg, Friedrich, 48
Tragic sense of life, 9
Turner, Frederick, 124, 125

U

Uncle Tom's Cabin (Stowe), 38, 45
Universality, 21, 22, 148, 149

V

Values, 23, 42, 63, 68
Verducci, Susan, 151
Violence, 25, 26, 38
Virtue ethics, 2, 5, 87
Virtues, 4, 6, 16, 22, 23, 40, 62, 65, 68,
        97, 103, 110, 123, 152

Vitz, Paul, 124
Voices from the Inside, 132, 142

W

Waerness, Kari, 56
Walker, Lawrence, 119
Walzer, Michael, 120, 121
Warrior model, 109–110, 113
Weaver, Richard, 66
Weber, Max, 64, 65
Weil, Simone, 17, 19, 29, 40, 41
Weiler, Kathleen, 52
Welter, Barbara, 52
*When Bad Things Happen to Good
        People* (Kushner), 34
White, James Terry, 3, 23, 62, 81
Wiesel, Elie, 34, 46
Wiesenthal, Simon, 47–50
Wilberforce, Bishop, 137
Wilshire, Bruce, 33, 72, 124, 126
Wilson, James Q., 149
Winthrop, John, 65
Womanhood, 109–114
Women
    alleged moral superiority of,
        55
    and care, 19
    and conversation, 128
    traditions of, 10, 22, 37–38, 51–58,
        95, 106–109
    and violence, 18
    and virtues, 103
Women and Evil (Noddings), 91
Woolf, Virginia, 55–56
Wyschogrod, Edith, 67

Z

Zeldin, Theodore, 54

About the Author

Nel Noddings is Lee L. Jacks Professor of Child Education Emerita, Stanford University and Professor of Philosophy and Education at Teachers College, Columbia University. In addition to 10 books—among them, *Caring, Women and Evil, The Challenge to Care in Schools, Educating for Intelligent Belief or Unbelief,* and *Philosophy of Education*—she is the author of more than 170 articles and chapters on topics ranging from the ethics of care to mathematical problem solving. Another new book, *Starting at Home: Care and Social Policy,* will be published by the University of California Press this year.

Please remember that this is a library book,
and that it belongs only temporarily to each
person who uses it. Be considerate. Do
not write in this, or any, library book.

DATE DUE

'JUL 0 6 2002		
AG 19 '02		
I LL	FE 24 08	
50\6\54	AP 11 '08	
4/28/03	SE 2 6 09	
JE 30 '03		
AG 23 '03	SEP 0 5 2010	
NO 10 '04	2/26/10	
MR 13 '05		
AG 29 '05		
NO 18 '05		
AP 16 '06		
OC 25 '06		
UE 22 '06		
AG 27 '07		